Eyewitness to

# A Redcoat and Greencoat at War:

The Narratives of Shadrach Byfield of the 41st Regiment and Thaddeus Lewis of the Glengarry Light Infantry

Shadrach Byfield & Thaddeus Lewis

Edited and Annotated by Michael Phifer

Works originally entitled:

*A Narrative of A Light Company Soldier's Service, in The 41$^{st}$ Regiment of Foot. During the Late American War; Together With Some Adventures Amongst The Indian Tribes, From 1812 to 1814.* &
*Autobiography of Thaddeus Lewis, a minister of the Methodist Episcopal Church in Canada*

Introduction and new material Copyright © 2013 Michael Phifer

All rights reserved.

ISBN-9781482584400

Other books by Michael Phifer:

Wolves From Niagara: Butler's Ranger 1777-1784

Lifeline: The War of 1812 Along the Upper St. Lawrence River

Gunsmoke and Lead: Canadian Born Lawmen and Outlaws in the American Old West

Gunfire Along the River: A Concise History of the Battle of Crysler's Farm, November 11, 1813

The Last Campaign: The Fall of New France in 1760

For the soldiers of the War of 1812

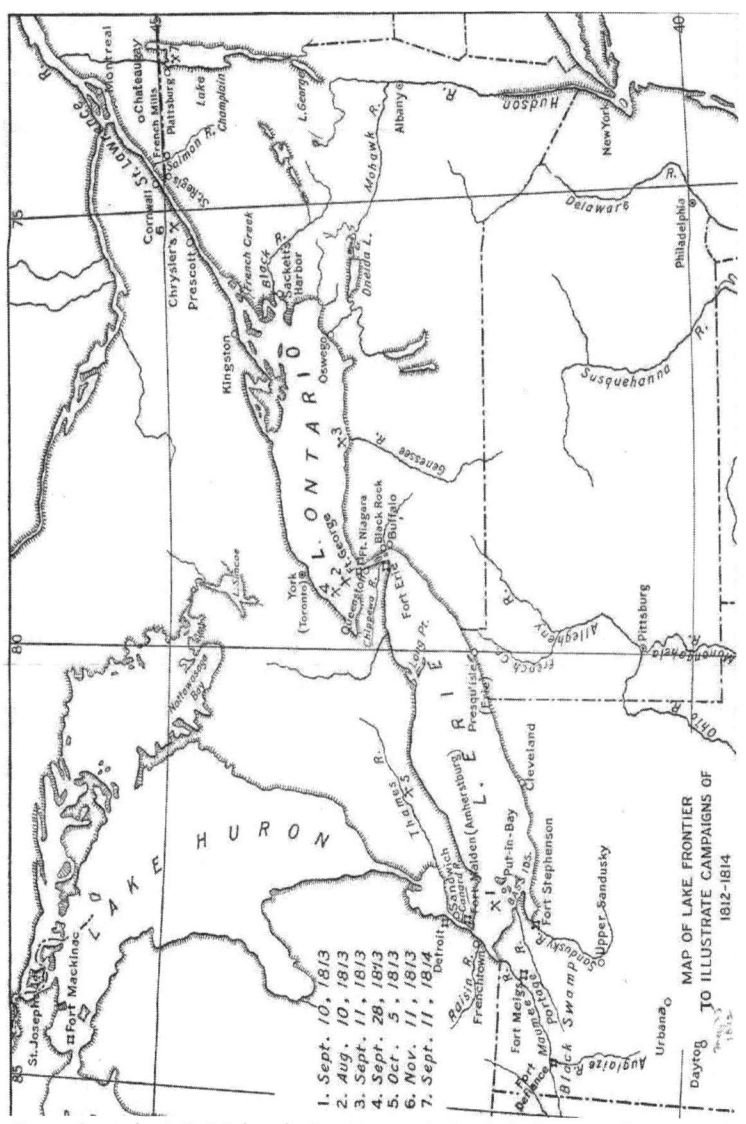

From Captain A.T. Mahon's *Sea Power in its Relations to the War of 1812.*

## CONTENTS

|    | Introduction | xi |
|----|---|---|
| 1  | Taking the King's Shilling | 1 |
| 2  | The Capture of Detroit | 7 |
| 3  | Fort Wayne Expedition | 14 |
| 4  | Frenchtown | 20 |
| 5  | The First Siege of Fort Meigs | 26 |
| 6  | Fort Meigs Again and Fort Stephenson | 36 |
| 7  | Disaster at Moraviantown | 43 |
| 8  | Drummond's Winter Campaign | 49 |
| 9  | Lundy's Lane and Black Rock | 58 |
| 10 | Returning Home | 67 |
|    | A Greencoat at War | 71 |
| 11 | Joining the Glens | 72 |
| 12 | Ogdensburg | 80 |
| 13 | Sickness | 88 |
| 14 | End of War | 95 |
|    | Bibliography | 98 |

# INTRODUCTION

Shadrach Byfield and Thaddeus Lewis have left us two wonderful memoirs of their experiences in the War of 1812 as enlisted soldiers at the "sharp end". Their memoirs are rare ones as there were not many written by the common British and Upper Canadian soldier during that conflict.

Byfield would see active service with the British Right Division in its successes and failures in western Upper Canada and in Ohio and Michigan. He would also see action in the Niagara theatre during the brutal winter campaign of late 1813 and early 1814. In the summer of 1814 Byfield would see hard service at Lundy's Lane and Black Rock where he was severally wounded. Through Byfield's memoirs we not only read of his experiences as a light infantrymen in battle, but also of his interaction with civilians, enemy soldiers and Natives. His attitudes towards Natives is of particular interest, as although the British and Natives often fought together to help defend Upper Canada, they did not always get along as seen in Byfield's narrative.

Lewis would see a good part of his service in the eastern part of Upper Canada. Although he would see action at Ogdensburg, most of Lewis's time in service would be being sick. As was common in the wars of the 18$^{th}$ and 19$^{th}$ century, the War of 1812 would see more soldiers die of disease or sickness then from enemy musket balls. Lewis's experience during the war would also be a spiritual one as he attempted to get right with God.

It should be noted that in editing this work I have not changed any of the text leaving in spelling and grammar errors. I have, however, broken up the bigger paragraphs into smaller ones in Byfield's narrative. (This was not done in Lewis's narrative.) This was done to make it more readable to modern eyes as Byfield's paragraphs ran on covering a number of topics.

I have also shifted Byfield's description of his experiences at the first siege of Fort Meigs in May of 1813 to after his experiences at Frenchtown in January of 1813. In the original text he has Fort Meigs taking place before Frenchtown which is in error. I have also added in square brackets additional narratives and memoirs of Byfield contemporaries who are describing the same event that Byfield is. This text is in *italics*.

In Lewis's narrative I have broken up one of his chapters into two chapters to make it easier to follow. It should be noted that his book is much longer dealing mostly with his life as a Methodist preacher. I have only included the chapters that deal with his experiences in the War of 1812.

It should also be noted that in Byfield's original memoir there were no chapters, but simply one long text. Again as with breaking up the paragraphs, I have broken up the narrative into chapters to make it more readable and to add addition material.

There are also footnotes in this work adding more information on the people Byfield and Lewis mention. The illustrations and maps were not in the original memoir.

It was with great joy that I annotated and edited this work and I hope the reader enjoys it as they see the War of 1812 through a redcoated 41$^{st}$ light infantryman and a greencoated Glengarry Light Infantrymans' eyes.

# 1
# TAKING THE KING'S SHILLING

I was born at Woolley, near Bradford, in the county of Wilts,[1] on the 16th day of September, in the year 1789, the day on which His Majesty King George the Third, came from Longleat to Trowbridge. I entered the Militia service in the year 1807. My mother on hearing I was enlisted (and having two sons before in the army) was so affected, that on the evening of the same day she fell in a fit and never spoke after, and I was obliged to march off the next morning; she expired on the third day after. Our route for Newcastle upon Tyne, where I joined the Wiltshire regiment of Militia.

After I had learned my discipline, the regiment marched to Norman Cross, to do duty over French prisoners. Those of us who were not perfect in our duty, were detached to Petersburgh for improvement; myself

---
[1] Wiltshire.

with others were soon returned to the prison, being considered fit for duty.

Our next route was for Ipswich, (Suffolk); I then got a furlough to go home to see my friends. After returning to my regiment, an order was given for volunteering to the line; a considerable number volunteered to the 41$^{st}$ foot,[2] and having a brother in that corps, I was one of the number: the volunteers soon marched for Portsmouth, and from thence to the Isle of Wight, in May 1809, embarked on board the Robert transport, and sailed for Quebec; we had a good passage, and arrived in about nine or ten weeks.[3]

While at anchor off Quebec, we received orders to take boats, and go up the river St. Lawrence; a few miles up the river, an aidecamp from the beach communicated counter orders, and we returned to Quebec, and occupied Jesuit's barracks. After having been there some time, a sergeant came into the barrack room, and asked if there was a lad who wished to be a groom to the quartermaster-general, I replied that I would go. Having dressed myself, the sergeant took me to the quartermaster-general, who asked me if I understood looking after horses, I said I did not, but that I was willing to learn, he replied, "You are the lad, I do not want one that knows too much," he appeared to take an interest in me, as he used to come himself and instruct me in cleaning the horses, &c., and ordered me to

---

[2] The 41$^{st}$ Regiment of Foot had been serving in Canada since 1799.
[3] That summer a draft of 210 rank and file sailed from England and reinforced the regiment.

Lower Town, to be measured for two suits of clothes; in the winter he went to Montreal, and took me with him, and understanding that I had a brother in the 41st, asked me if I should like to see him, as the regiment was expected at Montreal;[4] he gave me leave to wait his arrival, after which I was to return to Quebec without him, as he was going into the States for a short time.

While in company with my brother, Colonel Procter[5] enquired who I was, I being dressed in coloured clothes, he was told that I was one of the volunteers, come out to join the regiment; he ordered me into the barracks, where I received a suit of regimentals, and was ordered into the ranks. I felt very much hurt, being taken away from my master without his knowledge. When he returned from the States to Montreal, and finding that I was not gone to Quebec, he sent to the barracks for me. I waited on him, and he asked me why I had not returned to Quebec; I told him the reason, and asked him if he would wait on the colonel to get me leave to go with him, he said he should not humble to the colonel, but the clothes and the money he gave me I was to keep.

I was then put into the same company my brother

---

[4] The 41st had been dispersed in Upper Canada with detachments serving at Fort George, Kingston, York, Amherstburg, St. Joseph's, Chippewa and Fort Erie. In the fall of 1809 the whole regiment was ordered to Montreal where it was inspected by Major-General Gordon Drummond.

[5] Henry Procter (1763-1822) was born in Ireland and joined the 43rd Regiment of Foot in 1781 as an ensign. Rising through the ranks he became a captain in 1792 and a major three years later. Then in 1800 he left the 43rd to become a lieutenant-colonel in the 41st.

was in, (Captain Crowder's[6]). I had not joined the company long, when my captain asked me if I was a scholar, and when I told him I was not, he wished me to go to school, and said that he would make a non-commissioned officer of me; which offer I refused, being young and foolish.

Some time after this I was picked out for the light infantry company,[7] (Captain Muir's[8]). Soon after, the flank companies[9] received orders to go to Quebec, to form light and heavy brigades, where I had the pleasure of seeing my old master, who treated my very kindly; the brigade was broken up and we returned to Montreal.

[*Thomas Gibbs Ridout who was in Montreal at the time wrote to his father Thomas Ridout, the Surveyor General for Upper Canada, on July 3, 1811 on seeing the 41st there: ". . . the 41st regiment are continually out on the parade,*

---

[6] Lieutenant William Crowther (not Crowder) joined the 41st in 1806. He would serve with distinction at the battle of Queenston Heights and was later captured at Moraviantown. He resigned from the army in 1814.

[7] Each British regiment consisted of 10 companies, two of which where the grenadier company and the light company. The latter was often made up of spry young men who fought as skirmishers generally working in pairs so as to always have a musket loaded.

[8] Charles Adam Muir (1766 or 1770-1829) was born in Scotland. He joined the 41st in 1788 as a common soldier, being promoted to sergeant after five month service. He then managed to make the leap from enlisted man to an officer. In 1793 he was appointed adjutant and shortly afterwards became a commissioned officer being promoted to ensign. In 1794 he would become a lieutenant and see action in Saint-Domingue (now Haiti). In 1804, while with the regiment in Upper Canada, Muir was promoted to captain.

[9] Light Infantry and Grenadier companies.

*marching, forming, filing. They are 800 strong. I went on the parade yesterday afternoon, looking at them. The men made a very fine appearance, but I thought the officers almost too young." – Ten Year of Upper Canada in Peace and War, 1805-1815 p. 37.*]

After lying there about a year and a half, we received a route for Fort George; while here; several incidents happened in which my life was wonderfully preserved. One day, while standing on the quay, a sergeant who was ordered to York, on command, when going on board, his sword fell from its scabbard into the water. I heard him lamenting about it very much, and being a good swimmer I undressed, went into the water and dived for it, found it and brought it up; the sergeant was very thankful, and offered me any thing I would accept; but this act produced a fit of illness, (I being under water a considerable time) it affected my head.

Soon after my recovery, as we were on a fishing party, I was employed in holding one end of the net, and with the violence of the wind and the waves I was pulled into the water, from the ice on which I was standing, and came in contact with the boat, and was almost squeezed to death between the boat and the ice. I was pulled into the boat and carried to the barracks, very much bruised, but no bones were broken. Soon after this, we heard that war was proclaimed between England and America.[10]

---

[10] War was declared on June 18, 1812.

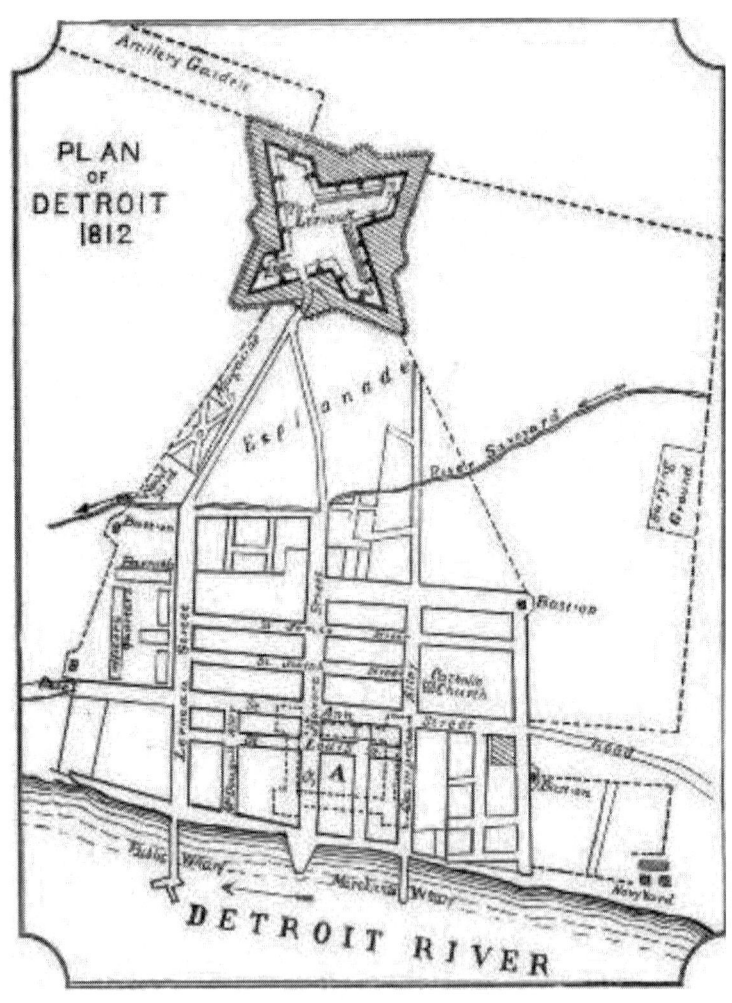

From *Richardson's War of 1812*

# 2
# THE CAPTURE OF DETROIT

One Sunday morning, being on sentry on the bank of the river St. Lawrence,[11] I saw a boat drifting down the river, without any person in it; a party of men was warned to go and bring in the boat. While the men were out, the Americans fired on them, which was the first shot I saw fired in anger.

On their return, General Brock[12] being informed of the

---

[11] The Niagara River, not the St. Lawrence River.

[12] Isaac Brock (1769-1812) was born on the English Channel island of Guernsey. In 1785, he became an ensign in the 8th Regiment of Foot. Five years later he was lieutenant and that same year advanced to captain. He then exchanged to the 49th Regiment of Foot. By 1796, Brock was a major and in 1797 rose to lieutenant-colonel. Two years later Brock would see action in Holland against the French and Dutch at Egmont op Zee. In 1802, Brock came to Canada with the 49th where he held commands at various times in Upper Canada and Lower Canada over the next nine years. In 1805, Brock advanced to colonel and two years later was a brigadier general. By 1812, Major-General Brock (having been promoted in 1811) was not only in command of the troops in Upper Canada, but was also the province's civil

transaction, ordered them out immediately, to bring in the boat, and said if they fired again he would open the batteries upon them; they went out and brought her in without any further firing. The general immediately gave orders for a large bank to be thrown up, in front of the American fort,[13] to preserve the town; every man went to work immediately, the general staying with us all night. As the flank companies did the duty at the government house, I was amongst them. Our general was very much beloved; he used to come out and talk very familiarly with us.

After fortifying the town, we understood that the Americans had crossed the river from Detroit to Sandwich;[14] to which place we were ordered to march. We proceeded to Oxford, and collected as many volunteers as we could, and from thence to Long Point, where General Brock met us with reinforcements. We then went on to Maldon.[15] The general there gave orders for every man that was fit for duty to march for Sandwich, and we left Maldon under his command.

The Americans had erected works, at Sandwich, but hearing that we were advancing, they burnt and

---

administrator. He was killed at Queenston Heights on October 13, 1812.
[13] Fort Niagara.
[14] The American Northwest Army under Brigadier-General William Hull crossed the Detroit River and took the little village of Sandwich in western Upper Canada on July 12, 1812.
[15] Fort Malden. The proper name of the post was Fort Amherstburg, but it was often called Fort Malden.

destroyed them, and returned over to Detroit.[16] When we arrived at Sandwich, the general gave orders to build batteries, opposite the town and fort of Detroit. When the works were completed, which was on Sunday morning, August 16th, 1812, orders were given for the batteries[17] to be opened, and about five hundred of the troops, besides a few Indians and volunteers, were ordered to cross the river, in boats, below Sandwich: our general was with us.

*[Brock would report to Lieutenant-General Sir George Prevost, the Governor General of the Canadas and commander-in-chief of British North America on August 17: "The force which I instantly directed to march against the enemy consisted of 30 Artillery, 250 41st Regiment, 50 Royal Newfoundland Regiment, 400 militia, and about 600 Indians, to which were attached three 6-pounders and two 3-pounders." - From Life and Times of Major-General Sir Isaac Brock, K.B. p. 162.]*

The Americans opened their batteries upon us;[18] we made our landing good, and marched towards the town. When we entered the field in front of the American fort, we were marched rank and file, and halted; the enemy at

---

[16] The American detachments still in western Upper Canada retreated back to Detroit on August 8 when Hull received word the day before that the American fort on Mackinac Island, located in the strait connecting Lake Huron and Lake Michigan, had fallen to a British and Native force. Hull now feared thousands of Native warriors would be advancing on him from Lake Huron.

[17] The batteries consisted of one 18-pounder, two 12-pounders and two 5 ½-inch mortars.

[18] The American batteries that returned fire consisted of seven 24-pounders.

the same time marched out of the fort, and formed in three columns; after a short time they returned into the fort again.

**Major-General Isaac Brock (Library and Archives Canada).**

Our general gave orders that all the spare jackets were to be given to the volunteers, and extended the lines as far as possible. After awhile an officer came from the fort with a flag of truce: General Brock came up to meet the flag of truce, with his attendants to the advance. I was on the advance with the general at the time, and from what we could hear, the officer wanted three days' cessation; to which our general replied, that if they did not yield in three hours, he would blow up every one of them.

[*Brock in his report describes the same event this way: "Accordingly the troops advanced to within one mile of the fort, and having learned that the enemy had taken little or no precaution toward the land side. I resolved on an assault, whilst the Indians penetrated his camp. Brigadier-General Hull, however, prevented this movement by proposing a cessation of hostilities, for the purpose of preparing terms of capitulation. Lieut.-Colonel John Macdonell[19] and Captain Glegg[20] were accordingly deputed by me on this mission, and returned within an hour with the conditions, which I have the honor herewith to submit." -From Life and Times of Major-General Sir Isaac Brock, K.B. pp. 162-163.*]

---

[19] John Greenfield Macdonell (1785-1812) was born in Scotland and came with his family to Upper Canada in 1792. In 1808, Macdonell became a lawyer. Three years later Macdonell became Upper Canada's attorney general. Macdonell was appointed lieutenant-colonel of the York militia and would serve as Brock's aide. He was killed with Brock at Queenston Heights.

[20] John Glegg of the 49th Regiment of Foot.

The officer went back with this message, and returned very soon, with authority to surrender the fort; the enemy, shortly after, marched out of the fort, and laid down their arms, and we marched in.[21] There was a party warned (of which I was one) to go through the fort, to see if any of the enemy were remaining in it; when I saw three American officers lying dead. One of the men told me that one of these officers said, before night he would wash his hands in British blood. We found two or three of the enemy remaining in the officers' apartments, they were about to destroy the colours of the 4th American regiment, but we took the colours from them; entering another room, I saw several men, and ordered them out.

Whilst walking along, I slipped, and nearly fell, one of the men said, "My dear man, that is the brains of a man killed with one of your shots."

[*Thomas Verches de Boucherville, a fur trader and merchant and volunteer on the Detroit frontier, who was also at the siege of Detroit remembered seeing the same gruesome scene: "We found four officers dead in the mess-room, their brains scattered over the walls. They had been killed by the bursting of a bomb during the bombardment. A number of soldiers had also been killed by shells and grapeshot." – War on Detroit: The Chronicles of Thomas Vercheres de Boucherville and The Capitulation by an Ohio*

---

[21] Besides capturing over 580 U.S. regulars, which were sent to Quebec as prisoners of war, and paroling about 1,600 Ohio Volunteers, Brock captured 33 artillery pieces and 2,500 muskets.

*Volunteer p. 110.*]

After we had got possession, and the prisoners were sent off, our general who was about to leave us, assembled the troops, and thanked them for their gallantry, saying that it would be a feather in our caps as long as we lived. Orders were then given to fire off the American's arms. After discharging many of them, we were obliged to leave off, and draw the charges, as they were so heavily loaded, some with a musket ball and nine buck shots.[22] But notwithstanding I thus shared in the dangers of this capture, I have received no share of the prize money;[23] two different payments have been made for Detroit, amounting to several pounds each man, but I have received neither: owing to the neglect of the clerk, or some other cause, my name was omitted from being inserted in the prize list.

---

[22] The American soldiers often loaded their muskets with buck and ball as described by Byfield.

[23] As with sailors, soldiers who helped capture the enemies supplies and equipment that would be used by the government were eligible for prize money based on the cash value of the captured material. The money was divided according to rank, with higher ranking officers getting much more than enlisted men.

# 3
# FORT WAYNE EXPEDITION

After this, news was received that the Indians had surrounded an American fort.[24] About 200 of us, under the command of Captain Muir, were ordered to march towards the Mawme Rapids.[25] We encamped for several days; we then received orders to march to Fort Defiance.[26] Part of us marched through the woods, the others, with the ammunition and provisions, went up the Mawme river in boats.

We halted one night, the next morning crossed the river; and marched on through the woods, until we came to a large open space; where we encamped. In the evening, Lieutenant Barnett came to us, and asked us for some provisions, as he had tasted none all the day. We

---

[24] Fort Wayne in Indiana Territory.
[25] Maumee (also called Miami) Rapids which are located in Ohio.
[26] Fort Defiance was built by the Americans in 1794 by Major-General Anthony Wayne during his campaign against the Old Northwest tribes culminating with the battle of Fallen Timbers.

being scarce, my comrade asked me what he was to do. I told him to give him some, as he was a gentleman and a soldier.

In the night we were alarmed by an Indian whoop; every man was instantly ordered to stand to his arms. In a short time, six Indians and an interpreter entered the camp, who informed the captain that they had been out as spies, and in the evening, whilst passing through the woods, they saw a light, and made towards it. On arriving near, they discovered five Americans[27] surrounding a fire; they drew near, and when the Americans saw them, they ran to their arms. They (the Indians) ordered them to give up immediately.

One of the Americans, who was an officer, asked them if they had any British soldiers in camp. They replied, "No." He then said, "We will not go with you, but you shall come with us." The Indians immediately surrounded them, and took them prisoners. While marching them, the officer was heard by the interpreter, to say to the men, "Kill four of the Indians, and make your escape;" upon which the interpreter ordered the Indians to kill four of the Americans, which they did; the officer endeavouring to escape, the interpreter shot him, whilst running. To convince out captain that what they related was true, they pulled from their girdle the five scalps, the officer's ears, and a silver-mounted dagger.

We were then ordered to lie upon our arms, and in

---

[27] Possibly Ensign Legget 17th U.S. Infantry and four Kentucky volunteers.

the morning we returned to Fort Defiance; crossed the river, and encamped.

The next morning we heard an Indian whoop. Soon after, the Indians brought in an American prisoner.[28] The captain asked the prisoner, who he was, and how he was taken. He said he was a quartermaster-sergeant, of an American regiment, and was out hunting for honey. The captain then asked him, how many men they had in camp, and how far they were off. He replied, about 9000, and that they intended to encamp there to-night, but that it was doubtful, as they had to cut the road, through the wood, for the cannon.

Captain Muir then said to Captain Elliott,[29] (commanding the Indians) we had better retreat, as quickly as possible. Captain Elliott replied, he would rather an attempt might be made, to cut off their advance. Our captain answered, "If we are exposed to one volley, I shall lose all my men, therefore, I think it adviseable to retreat," to which, Captain Elliot agreed. We then lightened the boats, by throwing the shot overboard, and retreated to Maldon.

*[Captain Muir in his report to Procter wrote of his*

---

[28] Possibly Sergeant McCoy from Charles Scott's regiment.
[29] Matthew Elliott (1739-1814) was born in Ireland and arrived in North America in 1761 and became a fur trader among the Shawnee in what is now Ohio. During the American Revolution in 1778, he went to Detroit and joined the British Indian Department. In 1796 he was appointed superintendent of Indian and of Indian Affairs for the District of Detroit, but was suspended in 1797 for poor account keeping of funds. He was reinstated in 1808.

*reasoning for ordering a retreat: "Soon after our arrival at the place [Fort Defiance] Colonel Elliot and I went to look at the ground, and on our return a prisoner was brought in by one of the Indians, who said that he had strayed from the army about four days before, and that he had not eaten anything, during that time. We then examined him respecting the army, and he informed us that it was commanded by General Harrison[30] as far as Fort Wayne, when he was obliged to return to the Wabash in consequence of some of their towns have been burnt by the Indians, and that as soon as he had quieted them he was to return to the command of the army, and bring with him the force he took to the Wabash. That during his absence the army was commanded by General Winchester;[31] he further said that the army was three thousand strong, consisting of the following regiments, viz.: Wells' Regulars, Lewis', Allen's and Scott's Volunteers from Kentucky, Simmerole's cavalry, 250 strong, and 150 mounted riflemen, with one six-pounder and 70 waggons. That they were short of provisions, but that they expected another army of the same strength to meet them at Fort Defiance which was to bring provisions for both armies, and four pieces of cannon, and that both armies were to*

---

[30] William Henry Harrison (1773-1841) was born in Virginia and became an officer in the military seeing service with General Wayne in the Old Northwest. He later became governor of Indiana Territory. During the War of 1812 he was appointed commander of the Army of the Northwest.

[31] James Winchester (1752-1826) was a veteran officer of the American Revolution and in command of the Army of the Northwest, before being replaced by Harrison.

have met at Fort Defiance on the 26$^{th}$ inst: and that it was generally thought it was intended on their meeting they should proceed to Detroit. During this conversation I recollected what I had been told respecting the number of Indians I should have, and as nearly as I could judge there were not more than from 320 to 330 present. I mentioned this to Colonel Elliot, and told him I considered it would be madness with such a handful of men to think of opposing an army of such a force; besides, it was running the risk of being completely locked in, without the smallest chance of success, or even escaping. He then told me that two of the Indian conjurers had dreamt that they should be successful that day, and that they were determined to fight. I then told him to acquaint the Indians, that I could not see the smallest prospect of success, but on the contrary, should I engage, the whole of the troops under my command, must inevitably fall. I was determined not to throw away the lives of so many men, and for no purpose. He then went to Round Head[32] and informed him of my determination. Round Head then came to me with an interpreter and urged the necessity of trying their success in compliance with the dream of the conjurers, and that at all events we might drive back their advance guard. I agreed that that might be done, but what would be the advantage, when while we were engaged with these few men we run the risk of being cut off from our baggage and provisions, and at the same time allowed the enemy to get so near that to

---

[32] Roundhead (1773-1813) was a Wyandot chief and supporter of Tecumseh.

*retreat with my troops would have been morally impossible. He then repeated that as to being surrounded and cut off we could easily prevent that by retreating through the woods. I told him that might answer for his people very well, but would not for mine, and that if he would collect the warriors and young men of his nation I would wait for them at the camp we left in the morning, and we might then retreat in a body. To this he agreed, and we commenced our retreat accordingly." - From Richardson's War of 1812 pp. 298-299.*]

# 4
# FRENCHTOWN

*[It should be noted here that in the original text of Byfield's memoir he has the first siege of Fort Meigs taking place before Frenchtown. The siege of Fort Meigs actually took place after Frenchtown so I took the liberty of placing in its proper chronological order. It is Chapter 5 in this work]*

Some time after this, we were informed that the enemy were at the river Reasin.[33] Orders were given to cross the river St. Lawrence.[34] We landed at a place called Brown's Town[35], and then proceeded for the river Reasin, with about 500 of our troops, and a few Indians. We had to contend with about 1400 of the enemy, under the command of General Winchester.

---

[33] The Raisin River is located in Michigan.
[34] Detroit River.
[35] Brownstown.

When within about two miles of the enemy, we encamped for part of the night; early in the morning, we proceeded to meet them, and under the cover of a wood, we approached near to them, unperceived; we formed the line, and had a view of them, as they surrounded their fires. While we were forming, the Indians marched so as to get round their right flank. We had six field pieces, which led on in front of the line.

We were then discovered, by one of their sentries, who challenged, and discharged his piece, which killed one of our grenadiers; we then gave three cheers, and the Indians followed, with a war whoop: the fight then commenced very warmly. It was on the 22nd day of January, 1813.

Before day-light, we had charged them several times, thinking that we were close upon their line; but our men were so cut up, that after every attempt, we were obliged to retreat to the covert of a rising piece of ground, with considerable loss. The men at the three guns, in our front of the line, were all killed or wounded, with the exception of one man. One of our lieutenants (Clemon[36]) received three or four wounds by musket balls; and a field officer, I think, a lieutenant-colonel,[37] fell, having received several shots, but was not killed, four of our men advanced to defend him, one of whom took him up, and carried him into the rear.

---

[36] John Clemow.
[37] Lieutenant-Colonel Thomas Bligh St. George of the 63rd Regiment of Foot was the inspecting field officer of the militia in the Western District.

As the day approached, we discovered that what had been supposed to have been the enemy's line, was a made fence, behind which they were sheltered, with holes in it, through which they fired at us.

[John Richardson, a young Upper Canadian serving as a gentleman volunteer in the $41^{st}$ was also at Frenchtown and recorded a similar experience to his uncle : "About two hours before day we resumed our march. On Friday at daybreak we perceived the enemy's fires very distinctly – all silent in their camp. The army drew up and formed the line of battle in 2 adjoining fields, and moved down towards the enemy, the Guns advanced 20 or 30 paces in front and the Indians on our flank. We had got tolerably near their Camp when we heard their Reveille drum beat (so completely lulled into security were they that they had not the most distant idea of an enemy being near), and soon after we heard a shot or two from the Centinels, who had by this time discovered us. Their Camp was immediately in motion. The Guns began to play away upon them at a fine rate, keeping up a constant fire. The Americans drew up and formed behind a thick picketing, from whence they kept up a most galling fire upon our men, who, from the darkness of the morning, supposed the pickets to be the Americans; however, as it grew lighter, they discovered their mistake, and advanced within 70 or 80 paces of the pickets, but finding that scarce one of their shots took effect, as they almost all lodged in the fence. Being thus protected from the fire of our men they took a *cool and deliberate aim at our Troops, who fell very fast, and the most of the men at the Guns being either killed or wounded, it was thought expedient to retire towards the enemy's left under cover of some houses. I was witness of a most barbarous act of inhumanity on the part of the Americans, who fired upon our poor wounded, helpless soldiers, who were endeavouring to crawl away on their hands and feet from the scene of action, and were thus tumbled over like so many hogs." – From Richardson's War of 1812 pp. 302-303.*]

About this time, my comrade on my left hand was killed. It being now light, I saw a man come from the fence, when I said to my comrade, "There is a man, I'll have a shot at him." Just as I had said these words, and pulled my trigger, I received a ball under my left ear, and fell immediately; in falling I cut my comrade's leg, with my bayonet. He exclaimed, "Byfield is dead." To which I replied, "I believe I be," and I thought to myself, is this death, or how men do die?

As soon as I had recovered, so as to raise my head from the ground, I crept away upon my hands and knees, and saw a sergeant in the rear, who said, "Byfield, shall I take you to the doctor."

I said, "Never mind me, go and help the men." I got to the place where the doctor was, who, when it came to my turn to be dressed, put a plaister to my neck, and ordered me to go to a barn, which was appointed for the reception of the wounded.

As I was going, the blood flowed so freely, as to force off the plaister. I now saw a man between the woods, and asked him what he did there. He told me he was wounded in his leg. I observed to him, that if I had not been wounded worse than he was, I should be back, helping the men. I then asked him to give me a pocket-handkerchief, to tie round my neck, to stop the blood.

He replied, "I have not got one."

I said, "If I do not get something, I shall bleed to death." He immediately tore of the tail of his shirt, and wound it round my neck. I then got to the barn, and laid down, with my fellow sufferers.

I had not been there long before the doctor came, and said, "My dear fellows, you that can, had better get away, for our men are terribly cut up, and I fear we shall be all taken." He rode away, but soon returned, saying, "My dear fellows, we have taken all of them prisoners." At which news, I exclaimed, (being quite overjoyed), "I don't mind about my wound, since that is the case."

While in the barn, I was much affected, by seeing and hearing a lad, about 11 or 12 years of age, who was wounded in one of his knees. The little fellow's cries, from the pain of his wound; his crying after his dear mother; and saying he should die, was so affecting, that it was not soon forgotten by me. He was a mid-shipman, belonging to one of the gun-boats; I think his name was Dickenson.

I understand, that while we were engaged with the enemy, the Indians pressed them on their right, and a part of the American force were sent to oppose them. The

Indians overpowered them, and killed a considerable number. Some of the Indians produced eight or nine scalps, each. This, no doubt, was one of the principal causes of the enemy surrendering.

There was a heavy loss of killed and wounded, on each side.[38] When we arrived at Maldon, there was a great muster of our men's wives, anxious to learn whose husbands were amongst the killed and wounded. The hospital would not contain the wounded, in consequence of which, some of them were put into the barracks. I was among the latter.

The next morning, I got my comrade to wash my neck, and shoulder, and I told him there must be something the matter with my shoulder, as I could scarcely lift my hand to my head. On examining my shoulder, he thought he could feel a ball, near the bladebone. I attended the doctor, and told him I had a job for him. On his examination, he found that the ball which had entered my neck, was lodged in my shoulder; he went to work and extracted it, and in about three weeks, the wounds were nearly well; and I was able to attend to my duty.

The prisoners and wounded were brought to Maldon, and, after a short stay, were sent down the country. Our light company received orders to march to Sandwich, where some of the company that had been detached, joined us.

---

[38] The Americans suffered 397 men killed and missing, while 547 were prisoners. The British had 185 soldiers killed or wounded, plus 12 officers wounded.

# 5
# THE FIRST SIEGE OF FORT MEIGS

After this, we were again sent to the Mawme Rapids, with two gun-boats and 11 or 12 pieces of ordnance, and landed about one mile and a half before we came to Fort Maggs,[39] on the opposite shore.[40] We then moved to nearly opposite the American fort, and began to erect batteries.

Our preparations were soon discovered by the enemy, and they endeavoured to annoy us, by opening their batteries upon us, but we persevered, until we had completed the works, with little or no loss, and then we returned the fire. We had a proof that our guns were doing execution, for one of our officers, with his glass, saw

---

[39] Fort Meigs, located in Ohio.
[40] [*This footnote is in Byfield's memoir.*] Fort Maggs is a strong fortification, on the American side of the river.

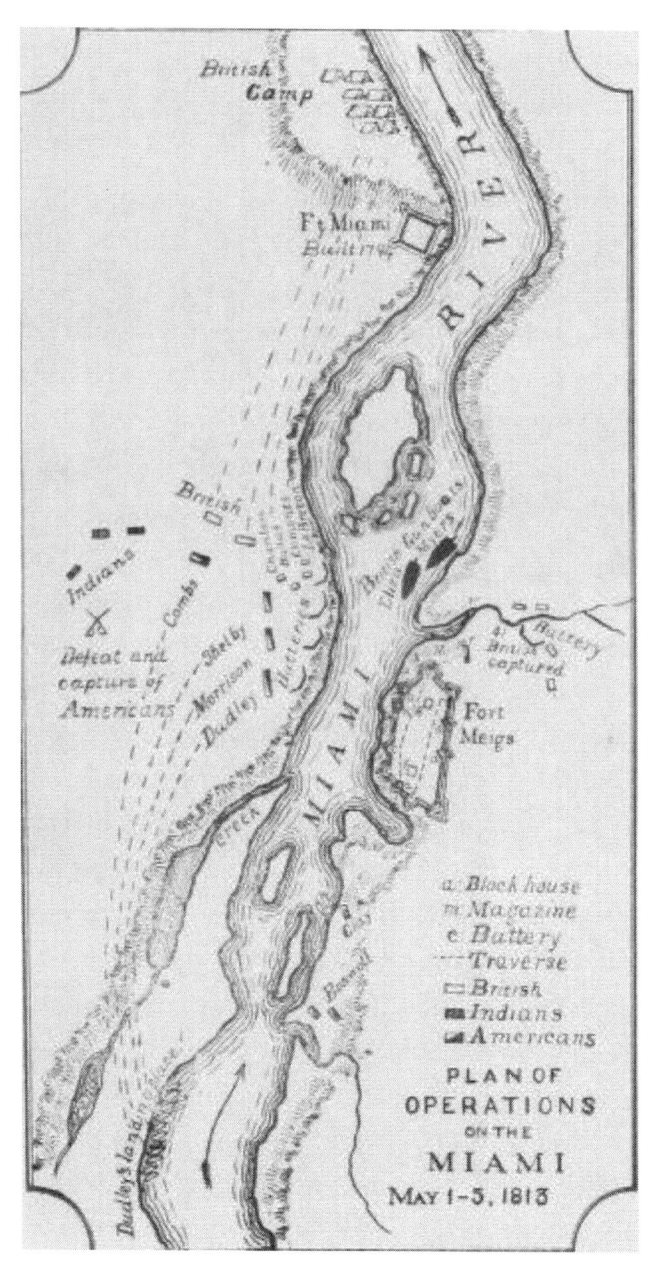

From *Richardson's War of 1812*

a man employed upon a building in the fort, he supposed he was covering their magazine with turf; this officer pointed out the man to one of our gunners, who took an elevation, and discharged the gun: the officer saw the man fall from the building.

Sergeant Smith and six of the light company, (I being one of the number) were ordered to dig a place, for to lay a mortar, in front of the American fort. The work being nearly completed, Sergeant Smith ordered me to go to the other battery, and let the artillery officer know, that the work was ready for the platform; and as I came up from the work, I looked towards the fort and saw a smoke ascend, and then fell to the ground; when a ball passed over me, and struck into the earth: I then went and gave the officer the orders, that Sergeant Smith sent me with.

A few days after this, the grenadiers and light infantry were ordered back to the camp, and from thence crossed the river with a six pounder and an howitzer, landed, and in the evening marched to within three or four hundred yards of the fort, and occupied a ravine, where the enemy's guns could not bear upon us, and by the morning we made platforms for the guns and howitzer, and commenced a fire upon the fort. Here we remained some days, and at night, sentries were posted in the woods, about 30 or 40 yards from the fort.

While lying in the ravine, one day, I went up to look round, when a ball came near my head, and struck a tree; I then looked round and saw an artillery-man shaving his comrade, the ball rebounded from the tree and struck the man that was shaved, in his head. He died in the evening of the same day, and left a wife and three children to mourn his melancholy fate.

One night, as I was on sentry, I heard a person coming through the wood. He accosted me, and gave me to understand that the Americans were coming down, on the other side of the river.

When I went off sentry, I acquainted the captain with what the Indian had said, who treated it very lightly; but about ten o'clock, the next morning, we heard a great noise and firing, from the other side of the river; on looking towards our batteries, we were surprised to see our colours down: 1300 of the enemy's troops had come down and got possession of the batteries, with all the ordnance, &c.

We then received orders to recross the river, and I and one of my comrades had orders to take a box of ammunition and throw it into a creek, to prevent its coming into the hands of the enemy. By the time we had done this, the enemy had marched out of the fort, when my comrade said to me, "We can stop here, we have no need to go back to the fight", but I replied, "What! see your comrades fighting, and not go back to help them: if you don't go back, I will shoot you." I hastened back, but cannot tell how he acted.

When I joined them, they were rallying for the charge. We charged them close under the fort, but were obliged to retreat because of their great guns, and were ordered to make the best of our way to the boats, to cross the river. Several of the officers and men were taken prisoners.

After crossing the river, we had orders to march towards the batteries as quickly as possible. When advanced about a half a mile, we met a party of our men, with a considerable number of the Americans, (prisoners), and were informed, that, on news being received at the camp, that the enemy had taken possession of the batteries, the whole force were ordered under arms and marched for the batteries.

Sergeant-major Keynes with 12 men, advanced in front, and when they came in sight of the enemy, they commenced firing. The sergeant-major was soon wounded in one of his arms, and lost several of his men, but that did not stop them, they were bold and courageous. The main force was not far behind, and very soon the fight became general, and continued for about twenty minutes, when the Americans surrendered, but some of them escaped to the woods.

*[Procter in his report to Prevost commented on the American brief capture of the batteries: " . . . I have the Satisfaction to inform your Excellency of the fortunate Result of an Attack of the Enemy, aided by a Sally of most of their Garrison, made on the Morning of the 5$^{th}$ Ins$^t$. by a Reinforcement, which descended the River, a considerable Distance, in a very short Time, consisting of two Corps of Kentucky Militia, Dudleys and Boswells,[41] amounting to*

---

[41] Lieutenant-Colonels William Dudley and William Bowell.

*1300 Men, under the Command of Brig$^r$. General Green Clay. The Attack was very sudden, and on both Sides of the River. The Enemy were for a few Minutes in Possession of our Batteries, and took some Prisoners. After a severe Contest tho' not of long Continuance, the Enemy gave way and excepting the Body of those who sallied from the Fort, must have been mostly killed or taken. In this decisive Affair, the Officers & Men of the 41$^{st}$ Regiment who charged, and routed the Enemy near the Batteries well maintained the long established Reputation of the Corps." – From Select British Documents of the Canadian War of 1812 Vol. II. p. 34.*]

We passed our men and the prisoners, and came to the batteries. The light infantry, and a party of Indians, received orders to go through the woods, in search of those who had escaped. I witnessed several affecting scenes in this pursuit. I saw one of our men, and one of the enemy, lying dead near together. I saw another of the enemy, that the Indians had met with and scalped, lying in a miserable plight, and begging for water; and while covering over his head with boughs, to screen it from the heat of the sun, a party of the Indians came up, and found fault with us, for shewing any lenity to the dying man: and one of them instantly dispatched him with his tomahawk.

We took several prisoners in the woods, and marched them to the camp. In this affair, a considerable number, on both sides, were killed and wounded. The prisoners being secured, and the detached men being come in, the Indians who had lost many of their companions, began to manifest a disposition to be revenged on the prisoners, and actually fired amongst them, and killed one of our men, who opposed them in their cruel intentions. Our officers interfered, and prevailed upon Captain Elliott, and some of their chiefs,[42] to put a stop to their cruel proceedings.

Tecumseh (Library and Archives Canada).

[John Richardson who was at the siege of Fort Meigs remembered the 41$^{st}$ soldier killed by the Indians: ". . . an old and excellent soldier of the name of Russell, of the 41$^{st}$,

---

[42]Tecumseh (1768-1813) who was born in Ohio and became a great Shawnee leader, played a big role in stopping the killing. When the slaughter of American prisoners was over almost 40 were killed.

*was shot through the heart while endeavoring to wrest a victim from the grasp of his assailant. - From Richardson's War of 1812 p. 154.*]

The prisoners were then put on board the boats, for safety, and put out into the stream. The flank companies were then ordered back to the batteries, where we encamped. The same evening, we heard that the American general had agreed to surrender Fort Maggs; and the next morning we were ordered back to the camp; and from thence we crossed the river, with a flag of truce, under the command of General Procter.

General Harris[43] came from the fort, with his attendants, and met our general, on the beach, who told him he was come to receive the fort, according to his proposal. The American general said he should not surrender; General Procter replied, "What! not fulfil your own agreement, that would be a violation of the honours of war," or words to that effect. He said he should not give up, for he knew his (General Procter's) strength, was far less than his own; and further, that he knew his strength, as well as he himself did. He was willing to exchange prisoners, and when that was effected, if they were not away in two hours, he would open his batteries upon them. It was thought that the American general gained his information, respecting our strength, from four men (volunteers) who deserted from us, the preceeding night.

We exchanged prisoners, and recrossed the river. We

---

[43] William Henry Harrison.

then embarked the ordnance, &c., went on board the boats, with the remaining prisoners, and sailed for Maldon. The enemy opened their guns upon us, from the fort, but we were nearly clear of them, and sustained no loss.

When we arrived at Maldon, we were employed, when off duty, under the direction of engineers, in strengthening and throwing up works. While here, one day, when on duty, a sentinel was wanted on board a vessel, and I was sent. (I relate this circumstance, to shew something of the cruelty of the native Indians, when they have it in their power). When I got on board the vessel, a person came from below, and was put in my charge; as we were walking on the deck, I entered into conversation with him; and as near as I can recollect, he related the following sad tale to me. I thought it deserved credit, for his feelings were much excited, and the tears flowed freely and plentifully. He said he had a small fortified place, where he and others defended their property; if I remember right, he said they were traders. –

"A party of Indians surrounded our place, and told us that the British troops were near, and would undoubtedly destroy us, and take away our property; but if we would admit them, they would protect us, and our property. Thinking that this reinforcement would be the means of preserving myself, my family, and my property, I consented, and gave them possession; when they began the work of destruction. They first killed my associates, and then cruelly murdered my children. Not satisfied with this, they took my wife, who was in a forward state of pregnancy, and murdered her before my face; they then ripped her up, and exposed the unborn infant, after which they took me off, a prisoner."

This was a very affecting relation; for hard and unfeeling as I then was, I could not help shedding tears, on hearing it, and seeing the distressed state of him that related it.

# 6
# FORT MEIGS AGAIN AND FORT STEPHENSON

We soon returned to Maldon again, and from thence, with a large party of Indians, went for Mawme Rapids, and landed about two miles from Fort Maggs. A plan was then formed, to draw General Harris and his force from the fort. A body of the Indians was placed in the woods, and directed to keep firing, as though two parties were engaged; in order to make the American general believe that we had fallen in with a reinforcement, which he was expecting; and endeavouring to prevent their joining him. We were in readiness to advance, and cut off his retreat to the fort, if he came out.

He came out from the fort, but the weather was tremendous, with thunder, lightening, and hail. We supposed that they suspected, or discovered the cheat, and returned immediately to the fort; as this project failed.

We returned down the river, to Lake Huron,[44] under orders for Fort St. Dresky.[45] We stopped at different places, and went on shore, to see if we could obtain any information respecting the enemy. At one place, we discovered houses and plantations, but no inhabitants, but in one of the dwellings, we found a dead body, partly consumed: we supposed this place had been depopulated by the Indians.

At another place, I, and some of my comrades went some way into the woods, where I had a narrow escape from a rattle-snake. I did not see it, at first. It was of great length, and size. When I saw it, I drew back. It appeared to be about to spring upon me; when one of my comrades shot it. We took it with us, and the Indians begged it of us, saying, that it was between nine and ten year old; and that some part of it would cure the bite of another.

We proceeded, and went up the river St. Dresky;[46] and disembarked on the beach. The following morning we marched for the fort. The Indians met with a man, and the officers tried him very much, to give some information respecting the enemy. He acted as though he was deaf and dumb, so that no information could be gained from him, neither by words nor signs.

The gun-boats went up the river, near to the fort, and we formed on a piece of ground no great distance from it. The enemy commenced a fire upon the boats, and us. The

---

[44] Lake Erie.
[45] Fort Stephenson located in Ohio.
[46] Sandusky River.

fire was returned from the boats.

General Procter sent Major Chambers[47] with a flag of truce, and demanded the surrender of the fort; or he would blow them up. He was led into the fort blindfolded, and received an answer from the American general,[48] for the commandant, that he would not surrender, and that he was ready to be blown to hell, at any moment.

We then took up a position near the fort, where we were sheltered from their fire; and in the night, made platforms for our guns.

The following morning, it was determined to storm. Our force was divided, and each party received orders, which part of the fort to attack. It was thought at the distance we were at, that it would be possible to scale the fence. We advanced in file, and formed near the ditch, and found it much deeper than we had expected; and the fence much higher. The light company, and part of a battalion company, were all that reached the works; the others were beaten back.

When the enemy found that the others had retreated, their main force was directed against us; and a dreadful scene ensued. Our men, generally, were determined. I saw one of them turn round, his comrade observed it, and said, if he did not face the fire, he would run his bayonet through him. We were exposed to the enemy's fire.

---

[47] Peter Latouche Chambers (1788-1827) joined the 41st in 1803 as an ensign. Three years later he became a lieutenant. In 1808 he rose to captain.
[48] Major George Croghan (1791-1849) was in command of Fort Stephenson.

My front rank man, the sergeant on my right, Major Short,[49] and Lieutenant Gordon,[50] were killed. My left hand man received six balls, but recovered from his wounds. We that remained alive, laid under the bank of the outer intrenchment. The officers and men in the inner ditch, were exposed to a swivel gun, and most of them were killed or wounded. I saw one of them come from thence into the ditch, where I was, wounded in his mouth, and the piece of lead lodged in it.

We remained in the ditch until night, when we received orders to retreat. Before this, I went down the ditch, amongst my dead and wounded comrades, to try to get some ammunition, as mine was expended.

I said to one of my comrades, "Bill, how bee'st?"

He said to me, "There is one of the Americans keeps firing upon us, out of one of those loop-holes."

I asked him to tell me out of which of the holes he was firing, and I would have a shot at him. He told me, and I fired. I had scarcely fired, when I saw my comrade fall back, wounded. I stepped to him, and said, "Bill, what's the matter?"

He replied, "They have shot me again."

By this time, the enemy had nearly ceased firing, and those of the men who could, were getting out of the ditch,

---

[49] William Charles Short (1767-1813) joined the 24th Regiment of Foot as an ensign in 1792. Nine years later he joined the 41st as a half-pay captain. In 1805 he advanced to major. In 1812 he held the rank of brevet lieutenant-colonel; the rank he held while killed attacking Fort Stephenson.
[50] John Gordon.

as quickly as possible; I do not believe there was either a commissioned, or non-commissioned officer left in it: and our poor wounded men groaning and crying, saying, "Now we have done the best we could, you are all going to leave us."

This the American officer heard from the fort, and said, "I know your men are going away, but never mind, my brave fellows, when they are gone, I will come out and take you in, and use you well."

I said to him, "Why don't you come out now, and we will fight you five to one."

He answered, "No, I shall not, but when you are gone, I shall come out and clear the ditch."

I then said to one of my comrades, "Now I shall start," and ascended the works. Just as I had got to the top, the flash of the guns caught my eye; I immediately fell on my face, when a shower of shot fell near me. I arose, and hastened to one of our batteries, when jumping into it, General Procter said to me, "Where are the rest of the men."

I said to him, "I don't think there are any more to come, they are all killed or wounded."

He added, weeping, "Good God!" What shall I do about the men!"[51] This was in September, 1813.[52]

We were then ordered to march to the boats. We went on board, and proceeded down the river, for Maldon. Before we came to the lake, we stopped and

---

[51] Procter had 96 British regulars either killed, wounded or captured.
[52] Actually it was on August 2.

went ashore. Here, one of my comrades, who was badly wounded, wanted to comply with nature's necessity, and asked me to carry him into the wood, for that purpose. My feelings were so excited, on account of the distressed state he was in, that I could not find courage enough, at the moment, to comply with his request; but one of my comrades took him up to carry him to the wood, and he died in his arms. We dug a hole in the beach, and buried him. After which we arrived at Maldon.

The flank companies were then ordered to Sandwich. This is opposite Detroit. When we took that place, in 1812, a circumstance occurred, which I here refer to.

An inhabitant of Detroit, a farmer, who, with his family, were in comfortable circumstances, having a loom, for weaving, in their possession, sent to enquire if there were any weaver amongst us. I and one of my comrades, being weavers, went to their house, and lent them some assistance in putting the loom to work. They behaved very kindly to us. I visited them often afterwards; and they continued their kindness to me during our stay there. The mistress suggested to me, that if I deserted, and went into the states, I should do well. I told her, I could not desert my colours; and, that I hoped to see old England again.

Soon after we came to Sandwich, I was one of a party, that was sent across the river to Detroit, for fuel. While they were getting it on board the boat, I asked the sergeant to give me a few minutes leave, to go and see my old acquaintance. I went to their former residence, but they were not there; the scene was changed. I found them in a cottage, reduced to a state of extreme poverty. The Indians had deprived them of all their property. The master was from home. The mistress said she was glad to see me, but had nothing to give me, but a piece of bread. I declined receiving it, and felt extremely sorry, to see them in such a state of poverty. Having five shillings in my pocket, I gave it to her; and have never repented it since. I then took an affectionate leave of her, and returned to the party.

On recrossing the river, with the fuel, we were in danger of being sunk, by getting enclosed in a shoal of ice, but we were preserved, we got clear, and landed, about half a mile down the river.

The flank companies were again ordered to Maldon. A party from each company were now sent on board, to do duty as marines; and the fleet sailed for Lake Huron,[53] to attack the American fleet. The action commenced, and we could hear the report of the guns, and were expecting every hour, to hear that our people were victorious; but contrary to our expectations, news was brought, that they were overpowered by numbers, and every vessel taken.[54]

---

[53] Actually Lake Erie.
[54] The Battle of Lake Erie (or Put-in-Bay) was fought on September 10, 1813 and was a disaster for the British losing all their six vessels either being destroyed or captured.

# 7
# DIASTER AT MORAVIANTOWN

Orders were then given to prepare to leave Maldon, and to take the ordnance, and all that we could, with us, but first to destroy the works, &c. In a few days' march, we came to 24-mile Bush, (or Moravian Town), and were informed, that the American general[55] was pursuing us, with three times our number, or more; and instead of using every effort to keep ahead of the enemy, until we were reinforced, we were detained in taking forward the general's baggage, &c.

It was said, that the Indians were inclined to make a stand, and endeavour to defeat the enemy, in order to keep possession of the upper country. The Americans gained upon us, and the Indians brought in some of their advance, (prisoners). A party was sent back to destroy a bridge, in order to check the enemy; while in the act, they

---

[55] William Henry Harrison.

were surrounded, and taken prisoners. Thus situated, we prepared to meet them, in the best manner that we could. The light company and the Indians were placed on the right, to face the Kentucky riflemen. We were thus formed, in a wood, when the enemy came within 20 or 30 yards of us, and sounded the bugle, to advance and attack.

The attack commenced on the right, with the Indians, and very soon became general, through the line. After exchanging a few shots, our men gave way. I was in the act of retreating, when one of our sergeants exclaimed, "For God's sake, men, stand and fight."

I stood by him, and fired one shot, but the line was broken, and the men were retreating.[56] I then made my escape farther into the wood, where I met with some of the Indians, who said that they had beaten back the enemy, on the right, but that their prophet[57] was killed, and they then retreated.

Moravian Town was not far from us, and the Indians wanted to know whether it was in the possession of the enemy, or not. They made for this place, placing me in front, and their interpreter asked me, if in case I should hear the voice of any one there, whether I should know it to be an Englishman's or an American's. I said I should.

When near the outside of the wood, I heard a voice,

---

[56] The battle was a disaster for Procter as he had over 600 men killed or captured out of roughly 900. Most of the these troops were from the 41st and most were captured. Byfield was fortunate to escape. Native casualties are harder to determine, but at least 33 were killed. The Americans had 29 casualties.

[57] Tecumseh.

Battle of the Thames (Library and Archives Canada).

saying, "Come on my boys," in a dialect, which I knew to be American. I communicated the same to the interpreter, and finding that we were discovered by the enemy, the Indians turned round, and made their way through the woods, as fast as possible; I followed after, as quickly as I could.

After awhile, they slackened their pace, and I overtook them; we went forward until night came on, when the Indians halted and formed round me, they seemed to be holding a consultation; I supposed it was to decide how I should be disposed of. In this solitary place, and surrounded by savages, whose cruelties I was somewhat acquainted with, I had but little hope, at the moment, of every getting out of the woods. My feeling on this occasion, may be more readily conceived than expressed.

After a short time, they went on, in Indian file, and I followed, until we discovered a light; I was then ordered to go on in front, to ascertain what light it was. I found an old Indian and a little boy, the old man being too far advanced in age, to go to war. They then came on, had some conversation, and stopped for the night. I wanted to gain their friendship, if I could, and having some tobacco in my haversack, I distributed it amongst them, and then laid down.

After passing the night, there, we proceeded through the woods, and after some time, discovered some cattle feeding. As we advanced, we came to an Indian camp, and after some conversation, between my companions and them, one of the females gave me some victuals, and spoke to me in broken English. I understood that she invited me to go with them, that is, with their tribe. I accepted the invitation.

The interpreter hearing it, called me aside, and asked me what I had been saying. I told him. He then told me, that if I went with them, I should go into the back settlements, and perhaps never come out of the woods again. This caused me to change my mind. I told the interpreter, that I wanted to find out some road or river, thinking that I should then find my way to some house or place. He then told me, that I had better go with him, as he should be in Quebec, some time in the following month.

The interpreter and three of the Indians then left the others, and I went on with them. We had not travelled far, when I observed one of the Indians give the interpreter a pair of moccasins, for the feet. I then thought that the interpreter had sold me, for a pair of shoes, and I shewed some reluctance to go forward. He asked me why I did not go on. I said that I should not, without him.

He replied, "You are afraid."

(I really was afraid, but did not want him to know it.) I answered, "I am not."

We proceeded through the woods until the sun had nearly set. I thought we were drawing near some road, I mended my pace, and was getting in front of them; when one of the Indians tapped me on the head, and said that if I did not keep back, he would take that off.

We went a little farther, and picked up a pumpion; in a short time after, I discovered one of my comrades. This was the best sight I had seen for some time, and my fears and suspicions, in a great measure, vanished; he had been wandering about, going he knew not where, and, no doubt, was as glad to see me, as I was to see him.

Soon after this, we came in sight of a public road, and by the road side we found some flour, some potatoes, and a kettle. We returned with the Indians, into the wood, and cooked it; we made a division of it, and found it very refreshing, being much needed. We stopped in the wood, that night; there was a heavy fall of rain, which made it very uncomfortable.

The next morning, we crossed the road, and went into the woods, on the other side; we forded several rivers, and in the evening, came to an Indian village. We were invited to one of the huts, and the head of the family was very kind, he killed a pig, and dressed it; boiled some Indian corn, and made soup; and entertained the whole of us, in a very friendly manner. We slept there that night, and, in the morning, I and my comrade took our leave of the old man, and our travelling companions, who directed us towards Oxford.

The same day, we fell in with a party of our men, who had charge of the general's baggage. We stopped with them that night, in the morning, I found that they were making too free, with what they had in charge. I was afraid of the consequences, and said to my comrade, "Let us push forward," but he was inclined to stay, and I went on without him.

I was ill prepared for marching, my shoes being entirely worn out; but before night I fell in with a larger party of our men, who had escaped, under the command of Captain Bullock,[58] of the grenadier company. He enquired how I had escaped. I related to him the particulars of what I had passed through. This party proceeded to Oxford, and from thence to the Cross Roads; where we remained for several months.

---

[58] There were two men by the name of Richard Bullock in the 41st. They were father and son. Bullock Sr. seems to have been promoted from the ranks like Muir having seen action in the West Indies in the 1790s. Reaching the rank of captain he was assigned to Mackinac Island in September 1813, thereby missing the disaster at Moraviantown. His son, who is mention here by Byfield, was a lieutenant and was one of the few officers to escape capture.

# 8
# DRUMMOND'S WINTER CAMPAIGN

From thence we marched to Burlington Heights barracks; and after a few days, to Fort George; the Americans having left it. Our flank companies, with the 100th regiment, were ordered to attack Fort Niagara. The 100th regiment was at Queen's Town;[59] we marched to that place, and joined them, and from thence crossed the river St. Lawrence,[60] and landed about four or five miles above Niagara. Generals Drummond[61] and Ryal[62] were with us.

---

[59] Queenston, Upper Canada.
[60] Actually the Niagara River.
[61] Lieutenant-General Gordon Drummond (1772-1854) was born in Quebec where his father was deputy paymaster general to the British forces. In 1789, Drummond became a ensign in the 1st Regiment of Foot and would see action in the Netherlands and Egypt. He came to the Canadas in 1807. In late 1812 he was transferred to Ireland, but returned to Lower Canada in early November 1813, but was ordered to take command in Upper Canada which he did on December 13.
[62] Major-General Phineas Riall (1775-1850) was born in Ireland and joined the 92nd Regiment of Foot on January 31, 1794 as an ensign.

Arrangements being made, we moved off for the fort; the 100th regiment was in front. On the way, we surprised a guard, at Young's Town; we took them prisoners, and obtained the countersign; but a man made a signal, by discharging a rocket, we supposed to alarm the fort: it had no effect, and the man was killed.

We advanced quietly, and a party, under the command of a sergeant, went in front. When he came near the outer sentry, at the entrance to the fort, he was challenged; he advanced and gave the countersign, seized the sentinel, and threatened him with immediate death, if he made any noise. He then proceeded to the gate, and was challenged by the sentry inside, he gave the countersign, and gained admittance, but the sentry cried out "The British – turn out the guard." Our force was fully prepared, and in a very short time, we had possession of the fort, with very little loss – December 19th, 1813.[63]

The 100th regiment was left in the fort, and we were ordered to Lewis Town,[64] which place was occupied by a small party of the enemy; but, before we got there, they had quitted the station, leaving one piece of ordnance. Here we were reinforced by a party of the 1st royals, from

---

Four months later he had risen to the rank of captain. By December he was major in the 128th Regiment of Foot. In 1804, Riall transferred to the 15th Regiment of Foot and saw action in the West Indies. In 1810, he rose to rank of lieutenant-colonel in the 69th Regiment of Foot. He arrived in the Canadas in 1813 and had risen to rank of major-general.
[63] The British suffered five killed and three wounded. The Americans had 67 killed and 11 wounded.
[64] Lewiston, New York.

Queen's Town; we were then ordered for Slustua.[65]

We were a little alarmed, in the evening, before we started; I was on sentry, and heard something like the movement of troops: it proved to be a party of Indians, bringing two men, belonging to the royals, who, they thought were about to desert.

We proceeded, the same night, for Slustua, (I was on the advance, with a sergeant's party) and when within about one mile and half of it, we fell in with an American guard. The sentinel challenged, and attempted to fire, but his piece missed fire. We forced our way into the guard room, where they were all in confusion; I seized one of them in a sailor's dress, and threatened to kill him, if he made any resistance. We made eight of them prisoners, the others escaped.

Our main force went on, and I, with some others, followed with the prisoners. We had not marched far, before we came to two roads; we took the wrong one.

Soon after, we heard some person coming behind. Not having a non-commissioned officer with us, I said to one of my comrades, "Go back, there is somebody coming," but he refused. I then said, "Take care of the prisoners, and I will go back."

I had not gone far, when I saw a man; I challenged, and he answered, "A friend." I asked him what he belonged to.

He said, "The Americans."

I ordered him to stand fast, or I would blow his brains

---

[65] Schlosser, New York.

out.

He replied, "I am a prisoner." I took hold of him.

He then said, "You are one of the men who came into the house just now; one of your men has got my boots; I am the officer of the guard."

I told him that I had a pair of shoes in my knapsack, and that he might have them, if he would. He said, that if he put them on, his feet would be frost-bitten – December 22$^{nd}$, 1813. I offered him some rum. He said, he did not expect to be so treated, if he was taken prisoner, and wept, begging that I would not let him fall into the hands of the Indians. I told him that if he behaved himself, no one should hurt him.

We now halted, thinking to remain until day-light, in order to ascertain the right road; we again heard some one coming; I went back some distance, and challenged.

I was answered, "A friend." I asked him, what he belonged to.

He said, "The British."

I asked him what regiment he belonged to.

He replied, "The militia."

Not being satisfied with his answers, I drew near to him, and took his arms and ammunition from him. A short time after, we saw another man, with polished arms, by which I knew he must be one of our men. I said to him, "You villain, what business have you got here."

He asked me, who I was, and said, he was as good a soldier as I was, and challenged me to fight. One of our men, (a jocular fellow), said to him, "You do not know who you are talking to, he is an officer, and will have you shot to-morrow."

I had a beaver hat on, and a silk handkerchief round my neck. (I had lost my cap, in the bustle at the guardroom, and found the hat; and was allowed to wear a handkerchief, on account of the wound in my neck.) From this, the fellow thought that there was some truth in what was said; and begged that I would not report him, but before day-light, he thought proper to decamp. He belonged to the royals.

When the morning came, we proceeded, and soon came into the right road. We found that our men had got possession of Slustua, which was a mill, and a place for public stores. The guard made some resistance, and the officer commanding it, was killed. I saw him lying dead, and asked the officer, (my prisoner) if he knew him. He said that he was a dear friend of his, wept over him, and said that he had been on parole three times. I then gave up the prisoners, and was put on guard, to prevent the men from making free with the liquors, &c., in the stores.

Orders were then given to destroy the stores, and to burn the buildings; some of the provisions were thrown into the river. When this work of destruction was completed, we returned to Lewis Town. Two circumstances happened, here, of a very serious nature. One of our men, went into the woods, and was murdered by an Indian. We manifested much displeasure respecting it. The tribe, to make an atonement for this act, caused the murderer to be killed, and exposed in the public road, for some days.

We were ordered under arms, one night, when one of our men, by his carelessness, caused his piece to explode, and the contents passed through his right hand man, and killed him.

From Lewis Town, we crossed the river, for Queen's Town – December 22$^{nd}$, 1813 – We marched up the lines, to cross over again, in order to attack Black Rock; and were reinforced on the way, by men from the royals, and 8$^{th}$ regiment. Our force was then divided. The royals went above Fort Erie, to cross the river above Black Rock; the remainder was to cross below Fort Erie, so as to land below Black Rock. Fort Erie, is nearly opposite Black Rock, on the opposite side of the river. We effected our landing, according to orders.

The first that landed, surprised a guard, commanded by a Major Cotton,[66] and took them prisoners. The line was then formed, and had orders to remain still, until morning, if nothing happened; and then to advance, on the firing of a gun.

We had not been there long, when a person came mounted, within 20 yards of our line, and exclaimed, "Damn you, Major Cotton, where are you, and the British landing."

General Ryal, being not far from him, said, "I pray, sir, who are you?"

The other replied, by asking the same question. The former answered, "I am a British general," and challenged

---

[66] Possibly Captain Salmon C. Cotton of 26$^{th}$ U.S. Infantry.

him.

The other said, "I am an American general."

General Ryal, then said, "If you are a man, and a soldier, stand before me."

He instantly turned his horse, and rode off in great haste.

The royals, in crossing the river, were carried by the violence of the stream, so far down the river, as to be exposed to the enemy's batteries, and suffered much, but they effected a landing.

Some time after this, the Americans came out of the town, and formed. We laid close and quiet, according to order, and heard the American general, say, "Make ready, present, blaze." Their shot took no effect upon us. We arose, returned the fire, and laid down again. As they did not fire again, we concluded that they had retreated.

We remained in our position until the gun fired, when we faced to the right; and having gained some ground, to the right, turned to the left, by sections; and advanced, until we came near to the entrance of the town, where we formed the line, on the first section. They fired upon us, as we were forming, and we returned it, as fast as the sections came into line.

The enemy soon began to give way. There was a heavy fire kept up, from a large building. A party of our men advanced, and stopped the firing, by taking possession of the building.

We now discovered, that the royals were exposed to their batteries, being carried farther down the river than was intended. We then directed our fire upon the men that were working the battery guns.

About this time, the enemy sent a party into the wood, to flank us on the left; but they were received by a party of our Indians, stationed there for that purpose, and were beaten back, with loss. They made an attempt to turn one of their battery guns upon us, but could not succeed.

As many of the royals, as survived, about this time, effected a landing. We now pressed the enemy very closely, and they began to retreat, for Buffaloe.[67] We got possession of Black Rock, and the Batteries, and pursued them to Buffaloe. I saw one of the royals, with blood flowing very freely from his face; I said to him, "You are wounded, you had better go back."

He replied, "No, lad, I'll pay some of them first."

The enemy made but a short stay at Buffaloe; they gave us a shot from a mounted gun, and retreated. We took possession of the place, being apprehensive that the enemy would get reinforcements, and return upon us. Orders were given to destroy both places, by burning; no dwelling was to be spared, except one, where the dead body of a child laid, who had been shot, in the street; this was in compassion towards the sorrowful mother. We stopped until the evening, refreshing ourselves, and burying the dead; and then recrossed the river, and marched down the lines, to Fort George. At this place, my brother met with an accident, which cost him his life.

---

[67] Buffalo, New York.

When our company was at this place, before the taking of Detroit, we were 110 strong, but now reduced to 15 men only, fit for duty; some of them had been wounded, myself for one. The other part of the company, both officers, non-commissioned officers, and privates, were either killed, wounded, or taken prisoners.

# 9
# LUNDY'S LANE AND BLACK ROCK

We marched from Fort George, to York, where the second battalion joined us – July 25th, 1814.

Our company, now filled up, was ordered, under the command of Captain Glue,[68] to Point Frederick, Kingston; supposing that the Americans would cross from Sacket's Harbour, and attack it. We remained here, until the weather broke up, and then returned to York, again.

About this time, the man who messed the officers, complained, that owing to the high price of provisions, he could not continue to do it, without permission to keep a canteen, and to be allowed a man to assist him. Permission being granted, he requested to have me; as I belonged to the light company, he was at first denied, but

---

[68] Joseph Barry Glew joined the 48th Regiment of Foot in 1798 as an ensign. A year later he was appointed a lieutenant in the 40th Regiment of Foot. In 1803, he gazetted to the 53rd Regiment of Foot. Glew saw action in Portugal and Spain, before transferring to the 41st in Upper Canada and advancing to the rank of captain in 1813.

it was afterwards granted, with an order, that when the company was wanted for any particular duty, I was to attend.

While at York, I went into the hospital, to see the wounded. One of the 8$^{th}$ regiment, who had lost a leg, said, "That's the man that saved my life," and related how, saying, that when he was knocked down, I had pulled him behind a tree, to shelter him from the enemy's fire. I recollected the circumstance; he was very kind to me, during our stay together.

Our regiment now received orders for Fort Niagara, to relieve the 100$^{th}$ regiment. While here, we were expecting the enemy, and were often under arms, all night, and the guns kept loaded, to receive them, if they attempted to storm. The light company was repeatedly sent across the river, to Fort George, as there was a force of the enemy in that quarter. The enemy made their appearance, but the forts were opened upon them, and they went back.

The flank companies were then ordered to Lewis Town, information having been received, that the enemy were in that neighbourhood. A field piece accompanied us, and the light company was extended into the wood, on the side of the road, to prevent us from being surprised, from thence. We found much obstruction, the enemy having blocked the way, with a large quantity of brush wood.

When we came near Lewis Town, we got a sight of a party of the enemy, encamped. When they saw us, they went off, in quick time, and left the camp, and their provisions partly dressed. We followed them, some distance, but they did not stop to face us, and we returned.

At this time, the British, on the other side of the river, were engaged with the enemy, at Lundie's Lane.[69] We could hear the report of their great guns. Our captain informed us, that he had received orders to cross the river, to assist them; and the grenadiers, with the field piece, were to return to Niagara.

We crossed, and landed at Queen's Town. It was at this place, that the much lamented veteran, General Brock, received his death wound, by a shot from an American rifleman. We moved from this place, in quick time, for about seven miles, and waited for orders, near Lundie's Lane. A noggin of rum was given to each man.

We then moved on for the field of action. We had a guide with us, and when we came near the field, our captain was called upon, by name, in a loud voice, to form on the left of the speaker. It being night, we could not discover what regiment it was. The guide positively asserted, that it was one of the enemy.

Our bugle then sounded, for the company to drop. A volley was then fired upon us, which killed two corporals, and wounded a sergeant, and several of the men. The company then arose, fired, and charged. They enemy quitted their position; we followed, and took three field

---

[69] Lundy's Lane.

Battle of Lundy's Lane (Library and Archives Canada).

pieces.[70]

In the morning, we collected the wounded, and received orders to burn the dead. One of the Indians persisted in throwing one of the wounded Americans on the fire, while living, although prevented several times; one of our men shot him, and he was burned himself.

At this fight, General Ryal was wounded, and himself, and his orderly, (one of the 19th dragoons), were taken prisoners. We were now ordered to join the regiment, at Niagara; but before we marched, General Drummond, personally, thanked us, for our conduct in the fight. The whole of the army, were thanked, in public orders, namely, the royals, 8th, 49th, 89th, and 103 regiments. The

---

[70]Lundy's Lane was a bloody battle with the British suffering almost 880 casualties and the Americans roughly 860.

89th suffered severely, in this engagement.

We joined our regiment, at Niagara, and, in a short time, part of the regiment, including the light company, was ordered to cross the river, to Fort George; and from thence, towards Fort Erie. In going up the lines, we fell in with our main force. We were expecting to storm Fort Erie, when orders were given, for the 41st, and part of the 104th, with a rocket party, under the command of Captain Perry,[71] to cross the river, below Black Rock.

While on the water, we heard firing, in the direction of Black Rock. We landed, and advanced towards it. When we were here last, there was a bridge between us and the town, over a small creek,[72] but the enemy had destroyed it, and on the inner bank, they had thrown up breast works.

They commenced firing upon us, we advanced, thinking to charge; when we discovered, that the bridge was gone. We instantly retreated, and remained until day-light; when a party was ordered to erect a temporary bridge, across the creek, and our company, and the rocket party, were to cover them. We stood some time, and some of our shot took effect. We saw one of the enemy fall, who was daring enough to get upon their works.

About this time, I received a musket ball, through my left arm, below the elbow. I went into the rear. One of my comrades, seeing that I was badly wounded, cut my belts

---

[71] Actually the British force attacking Black Rock was under the command of Lieutenant-Colonel John Tucker of the 41st.
[72] Conjocta Creek.

from me, and let them drop. I walked to the doctor, and desired him to take my arm off. He said it might be cured without it; and ordered me down to a boat, saying, that the wounded men were to cross the river, and they (the doctors) would soon follow. The party failed in erecting the bridge; and retreated with loss.[73]

When on the other side of the river, the wounded were put into a house, and the doctors soon came. They examined my arm, and made preparations for amputation; but after a further consultation, they told me, that although I was rendered unfit for further service, yet, if the wound could be healed, it would be better for my hand to remain on, if it was not much use to me, and that had better be first tried. I was then sent to my regiment, at Niagara.

After a few days, our doctor informed me that my arm must be taken off, as mortification had taken place. I consented, and asked one of my comrades, who had lately gone through a like operation, "Bill, how is it to have the arm taken off."

He replied, "Thee woo't know, when it's done."

They prepared to blind me, and had men to hold me; but I told them there was no need of that. The operation was tedious and painful, but I was enabled to bear it, pretty well. I had it dressed, and went to bed. They brought me some mulled wine, and I drank it. I was then informed that the orderly had thrown my hand to the dung-heap. I arose, went to him, and felt a disposition to

---

[73] The fiasco at Conjocta Creek cost the British 44 casualties.

strike him. My hand was taken up, and a few boards nailed together, for a coffin, my hand was put into it, and buried on the ramparts.

The stump of my arm soon healed, and three days[74] after, I was able to play a game of fives, for a quart of rum; but before I left the fort, a circumstance happened, which I here relate. There was a sentry posted near the wood, to prevent any of the men entering it, and we had to go near the sentry, for water. One of the artillery-men went on pretence of fetching some water, and when the sentry's back was turned towards him, he started into the wood, for the purpose of deserting, and the sentry (one of the 41st) shot him. The ball entered his body, and the wound proved mortal; he was brought into the barracks. His captain came into the barracks, to see him. The dying men charged him with being the cause of what had happened. The captain left the room, and he died shortly after.

My comrades, and the messman whom I had been serving, out of kindness and respect to me, made a subscription, of several pounds, and gave it to me. As soon as the wounded men were somewhat recovered, they were ordered, from the different regiments, to go on board the boats, used in the river, to go to Kingston, and in going down the river, we went on shore, by night.

On board the boat I was in, was a young man, a sailor, who had lost one of his arms, near the shoulder. I felt a kind regard towards him, and we became comrades. He was going down the country, to be cook, on board a King's

---

[74] Possibly Byfield met three weeks.

ship, the St. Lawrence,[75] 110 guns; he shared with me, the gratuity my friends had bestowed upon me. From Kingston, we proceeded to Montreal; and from thence, to Quebec.

One evening, after going ashore, I took a walk, alone, a little way into the country, and came near a large neat looking house, and seeing a lad, I asked him who lived there, he replied, "A three-handed man."

I said, "That's the very man that I want to see, as I have but one hand; if he should be disposed to give me one of his, we shall have two apiece." The lad said, that by a "three-handed man," they meant that he was wealthy.

After going a little further, I went into a farm house; the inhabitants of which behaved very kindly to me, and the mistress made up a bed for me, for the night.

When I came to Quebec, I met with some of my old comrades, who had been wounded, and taken prisoners. I was extremely glad to see them. They related the scenes, and hardships, they had passed through; and one of them, said he was left amongst the dead, his wounds were considered incurable; but he begged them to attend to him, for he thought he should recover. After remaining in that state, four days, before anything was done for him, they paid some attention to him. He was then, in a great measure recovered, but not well.

General Procter, being in Quebec, I waited on him, and asked him for a certificate, for the capture of Detroit,

---

[75] The *St. Lawrence* was the largest ship built on the Great Lakes. She was built at Kingston and was a massive three decker.

which he freely gave me; and told me, that he would give me such a recommendation, that I need not fear, but that a sufficient provision would be made for me. He asked me the particulars of the battle, at Moravian Town. I told him all the particulars I knew. He further said, that he was going to Montreal, and ordered me to call on him, before he went, or before we embarked for England.

Some time after, a woman told me that the general wanted me. I attended to the order, immediately, but the woman had delayed delivering the message. The general was gone, and I did not see him, neither have I had the satisfaction of seeing either of my officers since, although, I have made many enquiries.

## 10
## RETURNING HOME

We now had orders to go on board the Phoenix transport, and sailed for England. We had a tolerably good passage, but was a little alarmed, one night, by a sudden squall of wind. The sails backed, and we were near foundering, but in a short time, the vessel righted, and all was well. We landed in the Isle of Wight, and marched into Newport barracks. Dec. 1814.

After examination, we were sent to Chatham, by water. Having been passed by the inspecting officer, there, I was sent to Chelsea. I appeared before the board, and was ordered nine pence per day, pension.

My feelings were much excited, that day, on learning that our bugle-horn man, who was a young soldier, who had been but in one action, and had lost a fore arm, about the same length as mine, was rewarded with one shilling per day. I must say, that I felt very much dissatisfied with nine pence, and I made several applications, at different times, to The Honourable Commissioners of Chelsea Hospital, to augment my pension, but without success.

Hearing of a field officer, residing in the neighbourhood of the town where I live, and that he was a soldier's friend, I made bold to wait on him, and requested that he would be pleased to hear my case. He kindly condescended to comply with my request, and after hearing my statement, he was of opinion that I was not remunerated for my services, and loss. He, very kindly, said he would represent my case, and it was not merely a *promise*, he persevered, until he had caused an addition to be made to my pension, of three pence per day. For which, I very kindly thank him, and shall be ever bound, gratefully, to acknowledge his kindness to me.

Being deprived of my trade, in consequence of losing my arm in the service, and having received several very severe wounds, it was with great difficulty I could support my wife and children, in a respectable manner; my pension at that time, being only nine pence per day.

One night, I dreamt that I was working at my trade, and on awaking, I related my dream to my wife, and told her I could weave; she said, "Go to sleep, there was never such a thing known, as a person having but one arm, to weave," and on going to sleep a second time, I had the form of an instrument revealed to me, which would enable me to work at my trade. I awoke my wife, and told her the circumstance.

I went to a blacksmith, of the name of Court, and having drawn a design for him, on a board, he made an instrument for me, similar to the pattern, with the exception of some little alteration, which I thought was for the best, but which, on trial, I was obliged to alter to the shape I saw in my dream; and I am happy to say, that I have been enabled to labour for my family, and keep them comfortably, for nearly twenty years, in the employ of Edward Cooper, esq., clothier, Staverton works, near Bradford, Wilts.

The above is a true and correct account, as given by Shadrach Byfield, before me

## Edward Cooper,
January 1$^{st}$, 1840.

-----------------------------------------------------------------

I cannot but remark, that it is evident in the foregoing relation, that a kind Providence has preserved my life through the many dangers to which I have been exposed, and brought me back to my native home. And for what purpose? In order to manifest a further display of His goodness and mercy towards me, in convincing me that I was a sinner, and in high rebellion against Him, who is my best friend and benefactor. A conviction of this, has caused me to lay down my arms of rebellion; to sue for mercy, and to submit to his righteous sceptre. For the last twenty years, I have been fighting under the banner of a Captain, who has conquered every enemy, and defeated every foe, to my immortal interest. Although I have to contend with a threefold enemy, namely, the world, the flesh, and the devil, and am the subject of many imperfections, and rank myself among the vilest of the vile; yet I hope that my soul is founded on the eternal Rock of Ages, against which the powers of hell shall never prevail. And when I shall have to encounter the last enemy, Death; although he will gain a victory over my mortal part, yet I hope that my immortal soul will be enabled to shout "Victory," through the blood of the Lamb: and be admitted into the society of the blessed, where I shall be beyond the gun shot of every enemy, and landed safely on the shores of eternal rest; *where peace reigns*, and where war shall be known no more. Where a blessed eternity will be spent, in adoration, and praise to Him, who has redeemed and saved me out of the hands of every enemy.

## The End

[*It is thought that Shadrach Byfield died about 1850 or so.*]

# A Greencoat at War

Thaddeus Lewis later in his life from *Autobiography of Thaddeus Lewis*.

# 11
# JOINING THE GLENS

*[Thaddeus Lewis was born in 1793 along the Napanee River in Upper Canada. His parents were born in New York and had been Loyalists with his father serving in a Loyalist military unit. Thaddeus was raised in a Christian household with his father being a deacon in the close-communion Baptist Church.]*

In the nineteenth year of my age I enlisted for a soldier in the Glengary regiment of Fencibles,[76] in the British service,

---

[76] Initially a proposal was made to form a regiment raised from Glengarry County, Upper Canada in 1806 and again in early 1807. Lack of support in getting men to enlist in another unit, the Canadian Fencibles, dampened any idea of attempting to form an unit from Glengarry County and the plan was put on hold. In late 1811 the plan was reintroduced to the War Office. Both Brock and Prevost endorsed the plan in early 1812, which was accepted by the War Office with

this being the twelvth day of March, in the year of our Lord 1812, in which year the United States of America proclaimed War with His Britannic Majesty, George the 3$^{rd}$.

When I enlisted I had not the slightest knowledge of the War which so soon commenced. Now I was brought to experience new things, and pass through scenes which I never dreamed of. As there was a great number of recruits enlisted in the neighborhoods abjacent to Kingston, we were gathered to that post first, and as soon as sailing was practicable on Lake Ontario, there being a lack of sailors, I, with fifteen more of my fellow-recruits, was put on board a ship of War as marines, for an expedition to Fort George at the mouth of the Niagara River. Nothing worth inserting occurred on this voyage, only the merciful hand of God as in time past was still over me, and we safely returned to Kingston.

---

some modifications. Recruitment for the regiment was expanded to both Canadas, as well as Nova Scotia and Prince Edward Island. Recruiting in 1812 was greatly helped by Captain George 'Red' Macdonell from the 8$^{th}$ Regiment of Foot. Given the brevet rank of major, Macdonell with the help of Reverend Alexander Macdonell set out to enlist men into the regiment in the Canadas and especially from Glengarry County were they had clan ties. Other recruiting officers were sent out to recruit in various districts of the four colonies. In the end most men who joined the Glengarry Light Infantry did not come from Glengarry County and most were not Scottish. Command of the Glengarries was not given to Macdonell who was only to lead the unit if it did not reach full strength. Recruitment went well and command was given to Colonel Edward Baynes, Prevost's adjutant-general. Lieutenant Colonel Francis Battersby was second in command.

Soon after our return the body of recruits at Kingston, and elsewhere in the Province of Upper Canada received orders to march to a place called Three Rivers,[77] a distant of about three hundred miles from Kingston. But before we marched I took the measles, and now I passed through a severe calamity, for the ravages of that cruel disorder seized me in every part of my system, that was subject thereto, and what added to my suffering was that the most of my fellows marched away, leaving me and a few more of my fellows that were in like circumstances with me, and we had very little attendance, and I and some others could not get a place in the hospital, it being so crowded with the sick.

Now I was brought to think upon my past life, but blessed be the Lord, He was merciful and gracious to me and did not cut me off at this time, but restored me to a state of good health.

About the first of May of the same year, we having recovered from the measles, were ordered on board of batteaux, and we rolled down the River St. Lawrence, to Three Rivers, in Lower Canada, where we joined the regiment, after a safe arrival, by means of a well directed Providence over us.

But Ah! what a wretch was I, that I could be the recipient of the goodness and mercy of God; and not one expression of gratitude to Him proceeded from my heart or tongue.

Now I was brought again to experience something

---

[77] Trois-Rivieres, Lower Canada.

new to me, we were immediately put to drill and garrison duty, and these things proved too hard for such a constitution as mine, and I soon fell sick with a fever, and was carried to the Hospital, where I lay in much distress of both body and mind, for the space of about one month, this was a thinking time for me, and I took a retrospective view of much of my past life. O, how clearly did I call to mind the benefit of my Father's house; also the care and kindness of a living and tender mother, and the instruction I received in the time of my childhood and youth, this brought me again to see my wretched condition before God, as a sinner; I saw too his amazing goodness and mercy in that he had not cut me off, and hurried my poor soul down the steeps of irremediable woe.

Then I made a promise to lead a better life, and the good Lord in mercy raised me from a bed of languishing once more, and I soon became so strong that I returned to duty as a soldier.

Being now in health and among my fellow soldiers, none of whom made a profession of religion, I soon found myself running with them to the same excess of wickedness as before.

O, how did that blood that speaketh better things than the blood of Abel speak in my behalf. Truly I have experienced that God does not delight in the death of the sinner, but rather that he would repent and live.

In the beginning of Autumn of the same year 1812, we marched to Quebec, and about two months after we arrived in that city, we were again ordered to march to

Upper Canada. This was a matter of joy to me because I anticipated the happiness of seeing my parents once more, together with the rest of my dear and loving friends.

But this march dealt destruction and death to many of our fellow soldiers. For we set out with a great number of bateaux laden very heavy with ordinance stores and we had with us two gun boats.

The River St Lawrence being very rapid we were obliged to march sometimes from morning till night in the river, and a great share of the time we were wet to the loins, (like as stated by the Prophet Ezekiel) drawing the heavy laden boats against the stream. We began this march in the month of November and arrived at Prescott in the first part of December, and from this the reader will understand that the water was very cold, as well as the weather.

*[William "Tiger" Dunlop, a surgeon in the 89th Regiment of Foot, made the same journey a year later. He was a bit more fortunate as he did not have to wade through the frigid St. Lawrence River. The following is his description of the journey: "The journey was a most wretched one. The month of November being far advanced, rain and sleet poured down in torrents-the roads at no season good, were now barely fordable, so that we found it the easiest way to let our waggon go on with our baggage, and walk through the fields, and that too, though at every two hundred yards, or oftener, we had to scramble over a rail fence, six feet high; sometimes we got a lift in a boat,*

*sometimes we were dragged by main force in a wagon through the deep mud, in which it was hard to say whether the peril of upsetting or drowning was the most imminent. Sometimes we marched; but all that could be said of any mode of travel was, that it was but a variety of the disagreeable; so, as there was no glory to be gained in such a service . . ." – From Recollections of the War of 1812 p. 20.]*

We took our winter quarters at Prescott, and in the process of that winter we buried twenty-four of the front rank of the right flank company to which I belonged, all of whom died of sickness, and no doubt in consequence of that march, and the hardships connected therewith.

I too was brought very low and weak by a severe sickness, and although I was carried to an old log house which they called the Hospital where I had only some straw thrown down for me to lay on, and only my own blanket to cover me, notwithstanding all this it pleased God in his mercy and goodness to preserve my life and to restore me so that I was permitted to return to my quarters as a convalescent.

About this time my father heard of our arrival at Prescott; and came about eighty miles distance from home to pay us a visit, this was a matter of great consolation to me, I was not fit for duty but remained a convalescent till in the month of January 1813 at which time my father came to visit us again and brought my mother along with him, and in consequence of my not being able to do any duty, I obtained leave by furlough to go home with them.

O! what an amazing providence was here spread around me, for I do believe that the Lord here interfered in my behalf.

Had I have stayed there in that state of weakness, to which I was reduced, taking into account the nourishment and care that a soldier receives in such cases, it is not probable that I could have long existed in mortal life, and had I have died then, I could not have expected anything but eternal banishment from the presence of God, but mercy prevailed in my behalf. Glory be to God most High.

## 12

## OGDENSBURG

I returned agreeable to the limit of my furlough, and joined my company again at Prescott about the first of February, was restored to such health and strength that I immediately went to my duty as a soldier once more.

On the twenty-second day of the same month, we were ordered to cross the river St Lawrence on the ice and to attack the enemies fort[78] of Ogdensburgh, by storm.

We undertook the expedition very early in the morning and a horrid scene was before me. I do not feel adequate to discribe in full the particulars connected therewith, but the battle joined hard upon us, they being, as was afterwards understood three to one.[79]

Here were my fellows falling on my right and on my

---

[78] This old fort was a leftover from the French regime.
[79] Actually the British force numbered over 680 men, while the American force was less than half that number.

left, some dead and some wounded.[80]

Just before we reached the shore on the enemies side of the river, I received a shot a little below my ancle joint, which brought me down on the ice.

We were ordered to charge a battery with eleven great guns mounted on it, from which they were dealing out destruction and death to us, and we were at the charge when I fell, and while our troops were furiously engaged in charging them from the battery, five or six rifle men run out from behind a large stone building and took me prisoner and they took my rifle from me but left my accoutrements on me, and they put me into a large stone building which they used for a barracks where their wounded were, two Doctors were there and some women, mean time our troops had taken possession of, and manned their batteries, and in a short time there came a flag of truce from the British Commandent[81] informing the U.S. Commandant[82] he must give up the fort

---

[80] Lewis was with Captain John Jenkins of the Glengarry Light Infantry who was commanding the right column in that attack.

[81] George Richard John 'Red' Macdonell (1780-1870) was born in Newfoundland who's father was in the military serving there. In 1796, Macdonell joined the 55th Regiment of Foot as an ensign. Two years later he became a lieutenant and in 1805 transferred to the 8th Regiment of Foot where he became a captain. Three years later he was sent to Nova Scotia with his regiment. Brevetted to the rank of major in February 1812, he was again brevetted to lieutenant-colonel a year later, just a couple weeks before the attack on Ogdensburg.

[82] Benjamin Forsythe (c.1760-1814) was born in North Carolina. He initially joined the 6th U.S. Infantry in 1800 as a second lieutenant, but only lasted a couple of months with the unit when the army was cut back and he was let go. In 1808 he was commissioned at captain in the

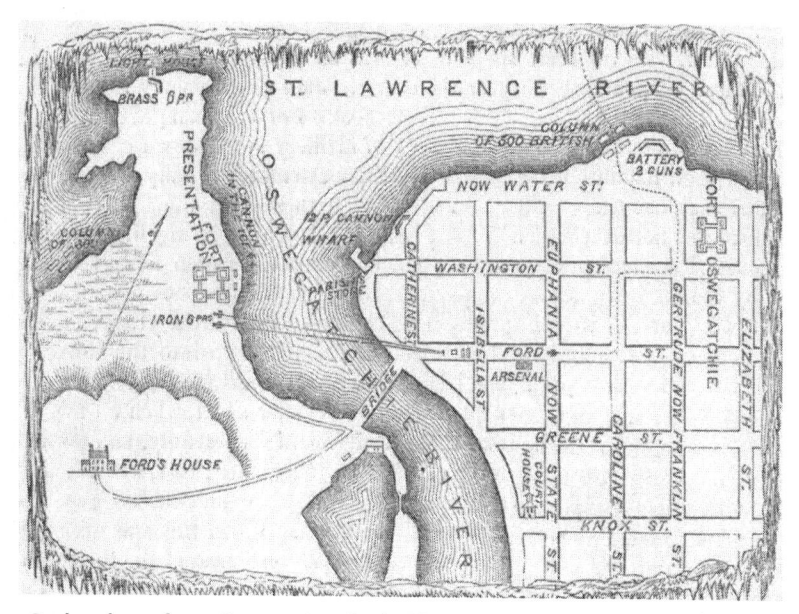

Ogdensburg from Benson Lossing's *The Pictorial Field-Book of the War of 1812*

with all its contents without delay, or he would put every man to the point of the bayonet. He replied that he could not (this I heard) give up the fort without more fighting. The British truce[83] having left, the U.S Commandent ordered his troops to make their way to a given point, ten miles off and not one to wait for another, and wait there till further orders.

The enemy at this appeared to be in a state of great confusion some ran into the building where I was to get

---

Regiment of Riflemen. In late January 1813, Forsythe was promoted to major and a couple weeks later promoted again to lieutenant-colonel.
[83] Militia officers Lieutenants Richard Duncan Fraser and Jonas Jones took the message to Forysthe.

their knapsacks, and by this means left some beautiful rifles and I took possession of one of them.

No sooner than the intelligence reached the British Commandant, that there must be more fighting before the Yankees would surrender, he ordered the British forces to load, and fire from every Battery, and every gun that was manageable, and direct their fire to that spot where we were and in less than ten minutes I was apparently in greater danger than every before, for according to orders our troops leveled all the artillery in the Town, and from the Batteries on that spot where I was balls and shot, of all discription, from sixty four pounders down, chain shot, grape and canister, came pouring in upon us, sweeping the street and shattering the buildings to pieces, and this fearful scene lasted about fifteen minutes.

In the time of the firing I had taken my stand in the Barrack room door supporting myself with one hand against the door post, and the other hand seized around the muzzle of the rifle, with the brick on the threshold; and as soon as the firing ceased, the staff adjutant[84] came down on the double quick march leading the division under his command, and seeing me in British uniform and having an instrument of war in my hand which belonged to the enemy, he supposed I had been fighting against the British, therefore he without any hesitation or inquiry, as soon as he got near enough seized me by the belts of my accoutrements where they crossed my breast, with his left hand and was that instant about to pierce my body with

---

[84] Possibly Lieutenant George Ridge of the 8th Regiment of Foot.

the sword he had in his right hand, but God in his providence delivered me by the only man in that division that knew me, who stood next to him caught his arm that instant in which he held the sword and stopped its force before it penetrated my body, and yet he tried again and again, to thrust the sword through me and at different times struck my body but my friend steady to his purpose kept a firm grip of the Adjutant arm until he drew my assailant and me out near the middle of the street, at last my friend cried out "my God will you kill the Colonel's Orderly." and immediately on hearing this he let me go. I was already very weak with the loss of blood.

Thus the Lord delivered me from death temporal and eternal, at this time, Glory be to God for his boundless mercy, at the time I saw the interference of Almighty God in my behalf, and while thinking of my wonderful diliverance I was laid on a cannon carriage on the top of several dead men and taken across the river again to our own side, and from thence to the Hospital.[85]

Here I had thinking time, I pondered with awful and yet pleasing delight on the goodness and mercy of God in spreading a kind shield over me in the hour of the greatest danger, and I thought too of my base ingratitude to God, and my continued disobedience to His commands, and the more I thought, the more terrible my former sins appeared unto me and considering the many dangers that God had delivered me from, and especially the one I had last

---

[85] In the engagement the British suffered about 70 casualties, while the Americans had 20 killed and wounded and 70 captured.

escaped, I was filled with astonishment at the amazing mercy and goodness of God, in sparing such a wretch as I, when in justice he might have cut me off long before, and appointed my portion where hope could never come. Indeed it seemed as if God by the Holy Ghost conversed with me by night and day. When I was awake the terrors of the Law were pronounced against me.

Now I promised the Lord to change my course of life, to break off from sin by righteousness. I wrote a letter at this time to my parents informing them of my deliverence from so great danger, and also of my resolution to serve the Lord and while I wrote I wept much, and in my imagination I roamed back to the place where my tender heart had received its earliest instruction.

Twenty days after the engagement the ball that I had received was extracted from my flesh, it lay in very deep. Under this operation I suffered much, notwithstanding in a few days I was dismissed from the Hospital and returned to my company as a convalesant.

I still felt resolved that I would not run into wickedness again, that I would shun such company as would lead me astray. But alas! when I returned to my old companions again, they set upon me to amuse them with singing of songs, which I refused to do, but the enemy of my soul laid a snare for me, when they saw that I was serious minded they plead with me only to sing one civil song, and they would ask no more adding that it would be no more than civil conversation, I complied with their request, and no sooner than I had finished the song than they turned their argument and told me that it was of no use to try to be serious there, and my conscience smote me for what I had done, to give them an ascendency over me, I lost my confidence before God and man, and I concluded it was of no use to try to be a Christian while I was a soldier, for the devil told me it was impossible to be a christian there.

At this time and under these circumstances it is impossible for me to describe the feelings of my heart, to give latitude to do evil as I had done, I dare not, without having something done, and what that something was I did not know.

However in this disordered state of mind; neither communion with God, nor fellowship with man, I came to the conclusion to promise God, that if He would spare my life until I was discharged, I would spend the rest of my days in his service and no sooner had I done this than the spirit of God left me to myself, and away I went again in sin and rebellion against that God that had given me deliverence in the most critical hour of danger.

Oh! the awful state of man by nature and alas! dreadful was my own state at that time; for had the almighty have cut the brittle thread of my life, and thundered me down to hail those infernal spirits that are now rattling their chains in blackest night, I must have owned the sentence just.

But how amazingly was the mercy, goodness and long suffering of the blessed God manifested toward me. O what is this that strikes my sense while I write these things. No wonder the redeemed sing a new song in Heaven, saying, "great and marvelous are thy works, Lord God Almighty; just and true are thy ways Thou King of Saints, who shall not fear thee O Lord and glorify thy name." Rev. XV. Chap. 3, 4, verse. My convictions having left me I think I ran more greedily into sin than I had ever done before.

## 13
## SICKNESS

In the month of May 1813, we with the rest of His Majesty's Forces in Canada were ordered to take the field; and encamp against the enemy. We marched to Kingston and from thence to the seat of war where our grand army lay at the cross road, about two miles distance from Fort George, which Fort was then occupied by the enemy who had taken it from the British a few days previous to our arrival at that place.[86]

We had suffered much on this long, and tedious march from Prescott to Queenston Heights, a distance of more than 300 miles, we travelled on foot carrying our arms, accoutrements and ammunition, together with our great coat, blanket, and knapsack two canteens and one havresack, with our provisions and kett, the roads narrow

---

[86] Fort George fell to the Americans on May 27, 1813.

and muddy, and part of the way no road, but through wilderness, and on that march we were three days in succession, without any provisions.

Our constitutions being over-taxed with fatigue some of our fellows fell sick, and I was among the number of them, and having being examined by the Doctor, it was thought best to send us to the rear to a place called Burlington Bay at the head of lake Ontario, about forty three miles in rear of the grand army.

When we came to take up our quarters at this place we were astonished, for we were sent there as a place, of clemency and safety; and on the contrary found the floor of our hospital to consist of the cold ground and its roof to be the canopy of heaven.

Weary and sick as we were there was no other alternative than to work, and make us huts of bushes in which situation I suffered much. The ague, and fever seemingly to the extent of its ravages, settled upon me.

After I had lain in the bush house with this disease for more than a month, and had became very weak, and without the aid of a physician or any attendance although I was a sinner against God yet he remembered me in mercy.

The officer that had the charge of us, himself being very ill at this time, hearing of my situation ordered that I should be taken to Ancaster to an Hospital, or if I could get a place in some farmer's house on the way I might with his consent be quartered there the latter of which I chose, and which Providence also gave me to enjoy.

About one mile from the camp a man and his wife

living near the road, readily and with apparent affection, accepted me into their house, here I found such, Hospitality and tender care as I had never found since I left my Father's house, and my sincere, and earnest Prayer is that God will reward them.

In about three weeks after I came to live with this hospitable family, the disease left me and having suitable nourishment, and proper care, I gained strength very fast.

I will just remark here that through all this scene of sickness, my mind seemed calloused to all spiritual things. I thought but little about the state that my soul would be in should I drop into eternity.

The comfort and care, afforded me in the kind family above spoken of did not be of long continuence; my health was restored, and I was ordered to duty again. There was still greater affliction awaiting me, for when the weather began to grow cold, so as to cause the armies to make their retreat from the field to winter quarters, we had to experience a voyage in bateaux on the open lake to Little York, now Toronto and from thence to Kingston, where we took up our winter quarters.

We arrived there about the middle of December in the year of our Lord 1813 now I was about thirty miles from my father's house, and I had a great desire to see my friends once more, and especially my parents accordingly I obtained a furlough limited to five days, this was on the last day of December, of the last mentioned year, but the suffering that I was about to pass through was hid from my eyes.

When my pass was signed I was in good health, as far as I knew, but in ten minutes after I was taken so ill that I could scarcely stand on my feet.

But being anxious to go home I pursued my journey and in the distance of the first half mile I do believe that I fell down forty times, so rapid was my whole system disordered, there I got an oppertunity to be taken with a sleigh five miles on my way, and there I was taken into a house in an insensible state, and in that state remained until the second day of January A.D. 1814, which was one day and two nights.

On the second day of January my reason returned for a short time in which time, I gave the men of the house to understand who I was and where I wished to go, and requested him to embrace the first opportunity to send me on about eight miles further towards home to a Mr. C's, which he accomplished that day.

Here at Mr. C's, I met with great sympathy, tenderness, care and hospitality. The next morning a sleigh was prepared with beds, pillows, blankets and sheets, in which I was tenderly laid, and brought home to my father's that day.

On the third day of January I was carried into my father's house in a state of insensibility and as helpless as an infant, although my mother, sisters and friends were attending me constantly, yet I had not any knowledge thereof, for several days.

In this situation, under the ravages of the typhus fever I lay twenty-two days, at which time the fever turned I began to recover, but was not able to leave my bed long at a time, until about the middle of March. While I lay sick as stated above, the Captain of the company to which I belonged had made repeated threats to send the soldiers after me. For this reason I was obliged to leave my father's house and my mother's care, when I was only able to stand the journey lying in a bed; this was a severe trial for a tender mother; and also for me it was cruel and severe, in the state of weakness I was in. When we arrived at Kingston I was carried into Block-house No. 3, my father and mother, having, performed their duty toward me, they returned home; leaving me in one sense in the hands of the hardened, and merciless; yet, no doubt, not without recommending me to the protection of Almighty God.

My parents being gone, I was immediately sent to the general hospital, and I had but very little expectation of ever coming out from there, until the flame of mortal life should be extinct. But glory be to the living and true God, "for his mercy endureth forever," he strengthened me both in body and in mind and gave me a speedy deliverance from expected death, "the way of Transgressors is hard."

But although I had been afflicted at different times almost unto death; I consider my deepest afflictions as mercies and blessings, compared to what I deserved.

Oh! what a deliverance was about to be granted me, while I write thereof I am astonished at the goodness and mercy of God, for not many days after I was carried to the hospital, there was a medical board ordered to examine the sick and lame, to ascertain how many, and who they were, that were not fit for the field the ensuing season; for the armies was ordered to march to the seat of war again.

When I was presented before the board for examination I was a horrid spectacle to behold, for when the fever left off raging through my system it fell into my right leg, and at this time it swelled in a shocking manner, and the hair had fallen from my head, like the leaves from the trees in autumn, and to make more hair grow, my head had been shaved by the barber of the hospital, this was done three sabbaths in succession by special order of the general doctor. I was emaciated to a mere skeleton and without hesitation I was one of those that were passed as unfit for service the ensuing season.

When I was reviewed by the Commanding General, by my request, he ordered that I should receive a furlough to go home to my parents, and just while I was talking with the General my mother and two sisters came to the Hospital.

I was immediately furnished with my furlough and returned once more to the parental roof, where I was nourished from the 10$^{th}$ day of May, A.D. 1814 to the 20$^{th}$ day of January, A.D. 1815, in which time I was restored to perfect health and strength, only the fever remained in my leg, which caused it to swell very much.

It was at this time, while I remained at home, that I first became acquainted with the woman that I afterwards married. O! I regret indeed that the time last spoken of was spent by me in great wickedness, such as Sabbath-breaking, profane swearing, and other accompaniments of a corrupt heart.

O! how great was the display of mercy in my behalf, in that I was delivered from the field of blood and carnage, where many of my fellow-soldiers suffered, bled and died.

# 14
# END OF THE WAR

About the 10$^{th}$ day of January, 1815, our Regiment having returned from the Seat of War, took up winter quarters in Adolphustown, about twenty-five miles from my father's; about the 20$^{th}$ of the same month I again joined my Regiment at the place above mentioned. My leg remaining swelled, I had again to pass an examination, and was passed unfit for further service.

I was told one morning by the Colonel that is was his intention to send me away in a few days to Quebec, and from thence to England, Chelsea Hospital, where I would receive a pension for life; this indeed was an inexpressible grief to me, it seemed to drink up all my spirits.

The thought of bidding a final adieu to my parents and other relatives pressed hard upon me, and what added to my grief, was because I had promised marriage to her who subsequently became my wife.

No sooner had I heard of their intention to send me away than I resorted to the canteen and took Intoxicating draught to benumb the feeling of my troubled breast. But this was a wrong course to pursue, to get rid of trouble. "The Lord is a very present help in time of trouble." Had I have paid my vow to the most high, and then called upon him he would have delivered me, and given me beauty for ashes, the garment of praise for the spirit of heaviness. But I sought death in the error of my way.

No sooner did one draught of spirits die within me, than I drank another draught, and down on my bed and slept on in this state of intoxication day after day. As near as I can recollect this state of things commenced about the first of February, and continued until the 22$^{nd}$ day of March A.D. 1815 which was about 50 days.

Had the alcohol of that day, been mixed with as much poison as it now, I have no doubt that I would have had a drunkard's grave, and I do believe, that if I had continued swallowing down the burning liquid one month longer I must have fallen a victim to king alcohol, and been reaping the reward of my crimes, beyond the reach of hope and mercy.

Here let me exhort and warn all those who are given to tippling, dramdrinking, inebriation in any way to break off at once and without reserve. Touch not, taste not, handle not: O! escape from this death dealing and soul destroying habit, do not say I cannot do it, you can do it, I did it at once; rally the whole man and with one effort, one resolution, crush the animal appetite *and be free*.

On the 22$^{nd}$ day of March 1815, the news came to us that there were preliminaries of peace, and I being one of them that enlisted for during the war I was aroused from a state of intoxication, by one of the servants of our company, who told me I must go with him to the orderly room, and have my discharge filled up, and said he, next day after to-morrow we will be discharged. The news appeared to me like an idle tale, notwithstanding it was true. Accordingly I was discharged from the British service on the 24$^{th}$ day of March 1815, and here my being a soldier, and my drinking alcoholic liquors to excess ended together.

*[Shortly after the war Thaddeus got married in July 1815 and settled down on a small farm. He and his family would later move a number of times in the coming years as Thaddeus would became a Methodist Episcopal saddlebag preacher. He died in 1866.]*

## BIBLIOGRAPHY

Antal, Sandy. *A Wampum Denied: Procter's War of 1812.* Ottawa: Carleton University Press, 1997.

Byfield, Shadrach. *A Narrative of A Light Company Soldier's Service, in The 41$^{st}$ Regiment of Foot. During the Late American War; Together With Some Adventures Amongst The Indian Tribes, From 1812 to 1814.* Bradford: John Bubb, 1840.

Byfield, Shadrach. *A Narrative of a light company's soldier's service in the Forty-First regiment of Foot (1807-1814).* New York: W. Abbatt, 1910.

Coffin, William F. *1812; The War, and its Moral: A Canadian Chronicle.* Montreal: John Lovell, 1864.
*Dictionary of Canadian Biography.* www.biographi.ca.

Dunlop, Dr. W.M. *Recollections of the War of 1812*. Toronto: Historical Publishing Co., 1908.

Edgar, Matilda. *Ten Year of Upper Canada in Peace and War, 1805-1815; being the Ridout Letters*. Toronto: William Briggs, 1890.

Haythornthwaite, Philip J. *Weapons & Equipment of the Napoleonic Wars.* London: Arms & Armour, 1996.

Hitsman, J. Mackay. *The Incredible War of 1812: A Military History.* (Updated by Donald Graves.) Toronto: Robin Brass Studio, 1999 (first published by University of Toronto Press, 1965).

Holmes, Richard. *Redcoat: The British Soldier in the Age of Horse and Musket.* London: HarperCollins Publisher, 2001.

Irving, I. Homfray. *Officers of the British Forces in Canada during the War of 1812-1815.* Welland Tribune Press, 1908.

Johnston, Winston. *The Glengarry Light Infantry, 1812-1816: who were they and what did they do in the war?* Charlottetown, Prince Edward Island: Benson Publishing, 1998.

Lewis, Thaddeus. *Autobiography of Thaddeus Lewis, a minister of the Methodist Episcopal Church in Canada.*

Picton: "The North American" Book and Job Office, 1865.

Lomax, Lieutenant and Adjutant D.A.N. *A History and Services of the 41$^{st}$ (Welch) Regiment (Now 1$^{st}$ Battalion the Welch Regiment,) from its formation, in 1719, to 1895.* Devonport, U.K.: Hiorns and Miller, 1899.

Lossing, Benson. *The Pictorial Field-Book of the War of 1812.* New York: Harper & Brothers Publishing, 1869.

Malcomson, Robert. *Capital in Flames: The American Attack on York, 1813.* Montreal: Robin Brass Studio, 2008.

Oman, C.W.C. *Wellington's Army 1809-1814.* London: Edward Arnold, 1913.

Phifer, Mike. *Lifeline: The War of 1812 Along the Upper St. Lawrence River.* Westminster, Maryland: Heritage Books, Inc., 2008.

Richardson, John. *Richardson's War of 1812: With Notes and Life of the Author by Alexander Clark Cassleman.* Toronto: Historical Publishing Co., 1902.

Turner, Wesley B. *British Generals in the War of 1812.* Montreal: McGill-Queen's University Press, 1999.

Wood, William. *Select British Documents of the Canadian War of 1812 Vol. I-III.* Toronto: The Champlain Society, 1920.

## ABOUT THE EDITOR

Michael Phifer, who lives with his wife Robin and their two dogs in rural Eastern Ontario, has written numerous articles on military and frontier history for such magazines as Military Heritage, Muzzle Blasts and other magazines. He has also authored books dealing with the American Revolution, the War of 1812 and the Old West. He is an avid blackpowder shooter and works as an historical interpreter.

Printed in Great Britain
by Amazon.co.uk, Ltd.,
Marston Gate.